Carl Hinder/Sell products

SALON PRODUCTS SELL OR DIE (NOT) TRYING

How to improve your customer service and beat your competition

Carl Hinder

Business Coach

Carl Hinder/Sell products or die (not) trying

Carl Hinder/Sell products or die (not) trying

This Book is dedicated to:

All the hair & beauty salons, barbershops, spas and clinics that have ever closed because they never grasped the concept of product selling in their business.

We are sorry to see you go, there really was no need.

Carl Hinder 2019

Carl Hinder/Sell products or die (not) trying

TABLE OF CONTENTS

TABLE OF CONTENTS	5
INTRODUCTION	10
PART 1: SELLING	16
UNDERSTANDING THE CONCEPT OF SELLING	18
PART 2 : WHY YOU SHOULD SELL PRODUCTS	22
PATHWAY TO SUCCESS	24
TO MAXIMISE SALES & PROFIT	28
TO IMPROVE CUSTOMER SERVICE	38
TO RETAIN MORE CUSTOMERS	48
BECAUSE IT IS GREAT MARKETING	50
TO REDUCE YOUR VALUE ADDED TAX (VAT) — UK MAINLY	56
PART 3 : WHY YOU DO NOT SELL	62
THE MYTHS AND THE EXCUSES	64

I AM NOT A SALES PERSON AND IT IS NOT MY JOB	66
THE PRODUCTS ARE TOO EXPENSIVE TO SELL	72
THE CLIENT DOES NOT HAVE ENOUGH MONEY	78
THEY CAN GET IT CHEAPER ON THE INTERNET	82
THE CLIENT DOES NOT LIKE ME BEING TOO PUSHY	86
I HAVE NEVER BEEN ASKED TO SELL	94
I DO NOT KNOW ANYTHING ABOUT THE PRODUCTS	98
WE HAVE NOT GOT EVERYTHING WE NEED	104
I CAN NOT AFFORD TO BUY THE PRODUCTS IN THE FIRST PLACE	108
IT IS THE CUSTOMERS FAULT THEY DO NOT BUY ANY PRODUCTS	112
PART 4 : HOW TO MAKE CHANGES	116

PRODUCTS	118
YOU NEED PRODUCTS	118
DISPLAYING THE PRODUCTS	124
PRICING THE PRODUCTS	128
FUNDING THE PRODUCTS	130
THE THIRD RANGE OF PRODUCTS	134
ORDERING THE PRODUCTS	138
STAFF	144
STAFF TRAINING	144
RECRUITMENT	148
THE CONTRACT & INDUCTION	150
TARGETS	152
COMMISSION & INCENTIVES	162
THE STRUCTURE	170
THE COMMUNICATION STRUCTURE	171
THE PRODUCT FLOW STRUCTURE	178

MARKETING	190
DIGITAL MARKETING	192
P2P: PERSON TO PERSON	196
PART 5 : HOW DO I REALLY SELL	200
THE RELATIONSHIP	202
EPILOGUE / CONCLUSION	208
BIBLIOGRAPHY	214
ACKNOWLEDGMENTS	216
ABOUT THE AUTHOR	218
SUMMARY POINTS	220
ACTION POINTS	222
SALES ORDER SHEET	227
CUSTOMER SERVICE RECORD	229

INTRODUCTION

This book is targeted at business owners and staff in the hair and beauty industry. This includes hair and beauty salons, spas, barbershops, clinics, stylists, therapists, cosmetologist, aestheticians, beauticians, barbers, technicians and anyone else in our industry. For the sake of ease, I will refer to the business as a salon, the business as a salon business, and the people that work within the industry as stylists. I appreciate the vast spectrum in skills and application. This book applies to you all, indeed it can largely be used by anyone in any industry that sells goods or services.

The fact that you now have this book in your hand tells me you are finally ready to start selling products in your salon. If I am wrong and you are not ready to start selling, then put the book down, give it to a friend or use it as a doorstop, because if you are not ready to learn how to change your business by selling products then it will not work. This is not a motivational, let us feel good book. If you think by reading this book it will endorse all the reasons why you have so far failed, or that this book will make you feel much better by telling you that you were right all along to treat selling like it is an option, it will not.

This is meant to be a hard hitting look at selling products, or otherwise known as product retailing. We will be calling it selling because I do not want you to hide away from the essential task which is selling a product. I do not want you to hide behind the words, education, recommendation and suggestion because if you failed to exchange money for a product and sell it, you are a little nearer to seeing your business failing.

It is not that every book, video or course on the subject is wrong, they are not, to the contrary, there is a lot of good material widely available for you to use. However, the attitude and approach that most salon owners, stylists, barbers and therapists take is definitely wrong. It must be wrong otherwise you would be selling lots of products, a lot less salons would be closing, and I would not be able to write this book. In this book I will talk to you about selling. You can be confident about saying it, say it aloud and get used to the word, SELLING. We do not need to call it a secret name, we do not need to disguise it like its word you must not use in front of the children, it is not taboo and you will not get arrested for saying it.

SELLING, SELLING, SELLING, it is your responsibility to the client, the salon and your family.

When you take this single business action you can increase your sales, your profits, your CUSTOMER SERVICE, your client retention, improve marketing and even tackle the dreaded V.A.T threshold (in the UK). Read that again, all these problems solved or improved by doing just one thing. What other single step can you take that will deliver all these benefits and almost for free.

Selling is not a novelty promotion, it is not an exciting new app or another social media tool, this is about understanding how selling is essential to both you and the client. Grasp this concept and I assure you, your business will change for forever.

OBSESSION

"NOTHING IN YOUR BUSINESS WILL REACH ITS POTENTIAL, UNLESS YOU ARE OBSESSED WITH IT. SELLING NEEDS YOUR OBSESSION."

Having had a number of my own salons, worked with many, many salons as a business coach and perhaps just as importantly had a career in the retail sector, I am always amazed and disappointed, that our industry, worldwide, deliberately turns away vast income from products.

Even more so, we reject all the benefits that come with selling products.

No other industry in the world would turn away so much of their potential sales and profits, it really does not make any sense at all. Salon owners would rather close their salon, underpay staff, struggle with taxes, not pay themselves and even deliver poor customer service rather than address selling.

An obsession with product selling is essential because it increases your customer service levels beyond the levels of almost every one of your competitors. In general terms, you cannot beat all your competition on the skills service, a haircut in one salon is largely the same in another salon, and whilst technically they can be worlds apart, what the client usually sees is not that different, and this is true with most services throughout the industry. You cannot beat your competition on price, certainly not for long. If you lower your price to beat your competition, your competition will do the same. A lower price just gives you less, it gives the client less, it gives the stylist less. It gives everyone less.

When a salon is selling a £/$300 haircut, or a £/$400 facial, they are not selling that process, they are not selling a product, they are selling the bit that you cannot always see, they are selling customer service.

Carl Hinder/Sell products or die (not) trying

> ## CUSTOMER SERVICE
> "YOU CAN ONLY BEAT YOUR COMPETITION ON SERVICE, YOU CANNOT BEAT THEM ANY OTHER WAY."

This book will reset your business thinking.

Carl Hinder/Sell products or die (not) trying

PART 1: SELLING

Carl Hinder/Sell products or die (not) trying

UNDERSTANDING THE CONCEPT OF SELLING

sell

/sel/

verb

1. give or hand over (something) in exchange for money.

2. persuade someone of the merits of:

Oxford dictionary

Almost every person in our industry will have an objection to the word selling. They will tell you that they did not get into the industry to sell, they came into the industry to make people look and feel great. They do not like selling, they do not like how it makes them feel and how it makes their customer feel. They are not good at it, and they have never done it. They will reassure themselves that if a client wanted it, the client would ask for it!

I am certain that some, if not all, of that sounds familiar to you. I am of course largely talking about the sale of retail products, but the same ethos can often extend to re-booking, upselling a service or just using the referral system.

It seems we have tunnel vison, bordering on blindness when it comes to identifying how a salon business exists.

A business has to sell.

All the general excuses are in one way or another either untrue or misguided. Stylists take them as truth because they are poorly trained and under educated, or the excuses suit their lazy attitude to customer service. Ironically, everyone sells, we sell something every day. We are just so natural at it that we do not even know we are doing it. It is only when we rationalise the process that we find ourselves unable, or more often unwilling to sell.

SELLING IS NATURAL

"YOU SELL YOUR VIEWS AND OPINIONS EVERY DAY TO GET YOUR OWN WAY IN LIFE."

Think about your life, at some stage you have probably gone out into the world to find a partner, at a local club or bar maybe. Before you left home you dressed smartly, probably styled your hair, or maybe even added a little make-up. When you arrived, you might have hung out in the area where there were lots of people, danced on the floor or sat at the bar.

Carl Hinder/Sell products or die (not) trying

You smiled at others and spoke in a manner that was pleasant to the recipient, you showed an interest in them and in the conversation, maybe you exchanged telephone numbers, followed each other on social media or even went for a walk down the beach hand in hand and maybe you closed the deal.

Perhaps you have gone for a job interview or maybe you have been to see the bank manager or financial advisor for a mortgage. You spent hours at home practicing interview questions, researching on the internet, completing forms and getting prepared to ensure that when you engage with the other person you get the best possible outcome. You listen to the other person, smile, make eye contact, answer their questions and present your case. You try and tell them what they want to hear, you tell them all the best things about you and convince them that you are the best person they could possibly find. You were always selling yourself. You really can sell.

You sold because you either wanted to or because you had to. These reasons push you every day to sell yourself, now you need to apply the same reasons to your product sales and customer service.

PART 2: WHY YOU SHOULD SELL PRODUCTS

PATHWAY TO SUCCESS

The short answer is because it solves a whole list of salon problems. What kind of a salon owner or stylist/technician does not want to have less problems? After thirty-two years of retail management, salon ownership and business coaching I have never had anyone call me up and ask me to help them get more problems. I would be very excited if they did because problems sometimes come as part of development and growth too, and we accept these as opportunities. However, I am still sure most people would prefer to manage problems than be managed by them. This desired state of normal problem free life makes it even more incredible that salons and staff refuse to sell products even though it reduces, and in some cases solves all of their main business problems.

This is the nearest thing to a magic wand that you have available.

So here is the challenge: you must change the way you see product sales. You have to dismiss all the nonsense reasons that you have grown up with in the industry for not selling, and replace them with common sense business reasons for selling.

This will not be easy, as the industry is entrenched in half a century of service versus selling (retail) propaganda.

Propaganda

Noun

- 1.information, especially of a biased or misleading nature, used to promote or publicise a political cause or point of view:

Oxford dictionary

By its own definition, the content of propaganda does not exist. You must realise and accept that service and selling (retail) are the same thing.

> ## SELLING IS SERVICE
> "PRODUCT SALES CANNOT BE OPTIONAL, UNLESS GIVING GREAT CUSTOMER SERVICE IS ALSO OPTIONAL."

You are up against a wall of product negativity, that is somehow passed on from one generation of stylists to the next. The belief that product sales are "optional" is being passed on in an almost cult like fashion and followed like it is "the truth, the whole truth and nothing but the truth". Except it is just not true.

Carl Hinder/Sell products or die (not) trying

You must inwardly and outwardly declare that not selling products is unacceptable. You must go from the hidden position "I will allow" my salon to not sell products, to an uncompromising, "I will never allow" myself or my team to fail in selling products.

If you buy into what I am telling you, you will find yourself "unable to allow" product sales failure, knowing it is at the core of your financial business. If you are a stylist/technician, you will find yourself "unable to allow" product sales failure knowing that it is at the core of your customer service. When you get to the position of being UNABLE to accept product sales failure you will have dismissed all the barriers and be on the way to greater success.

Carl Hinder/Sell products or die (not) trying

TO MAXIMISE SALES & PROFIT

The main reason your business exists.

If you are a salon owner, and you have to seriously consider whether Sales and Profits are important, then you are never likely to sell products or have a financially successful business. Ever. Your salon problems are almost certainly worse than just addressing the product and customer service standards and you need urgent business life support.

Stop reading and e mail me instead info@salon-help.co.uk

For everyone else, the number one reason for your business existence, is to maximise sales and profits, even if you have some kind of utopian lifestyle plan, you are going to struggle to do it without sales and profits. If you are not an owner but still work in a salon, then it is equally important to you that the business is growing and flourishing, you will get rewarded in so many ways.

> **SALES**
> "IF YOU CANNOT GENERATE ENOUGH SALES, YOU WILL NEVER HAVE A SUCCESSFUL BUSINESS."

It logically follows that if everything leads back to sales and profits, then do so products. This is a pretty simple and straight forward concept, at least for almost every other commercial business in the world. I am almost paralysed, mouth agape by the constant stream of salons that would rather close their business down permanently than take the opportunity of retailing products in their business. Maybe they are the lucky ones, as streams of salon owners go unpaid/underpaid every week, staff leave because they feel underpaid or not invested in, owners stress over the thought of another VAT or TAX bill heading their way, the pain goes on and on and salons will still not sell products, even though it will change their life. It might be too late for some of them, but you are reading this book and you can change your business today.

Source of data www.salon-help.co.uk

40% of Salons make a loss or break even every year (Often with a partner or other job contributing)

20% of Salons make a profit by operating around the law (avoiding taxes through subduing sales or using unconventional employment means)

30% of Salons make some profit but often with no long-term financial security or investment.

Some are retail focused.

10% of Salons have substantial sales and profits. Almost all are retail focused.

This indicates to me that up to 90% of salons are prepared to under-perform financially.

If you are breaking even, then you are making a loss. If you are breaking even, then you are going backwards. If your growth is so small that you are standing still you are always going to make a loss as everything else will be increasing. Your costs could be increasing by 10% a year, if your sales are staying the same you are making a loss.

MAKE A PROFIT

"IF YOU ARE BREAKING EVEN TODAY, YOU ARE MAKING A LOSS TOMORROW."

According to the 2018 National hairdressers Federation (including beauty) and the National Barbers Federation Survey, 38% of salons in the UK take less than £/$150,000 per year. They also have between one and six employees.

So, a typical salon taking less than £/$150,000 a year is unlikely to be doing well with retail sales. However, let us look at the potential impact on a salon for each full-time employee, who decides to sell.

Hair & Beauty Salon - Average product price £/$ 15.00

Assuming that each stylist does 8 clients a day and works 5 days per week. That stylist does 40 clients per week

If the stylist converts (sells) to 40% of these clients that would be 16 clients per week.

16 clients paying £/$ 15.00 each = £/$ 240.00 a week

If they did that every week of the year that would equal **£/$ 12,480.00 in sales per year**

1 Stylist	=	£/$12,480.00
2 Stylists	=	£/$ 24,960.00
3 Stylists	=	£/$ 37,440.00
4 Stylists	=	£/$ 49,920.00
5 Stylists	=	£/$ 62,400.00
6 Stylists	=	£/$ 74.880.00

However, I believe that this is still underperforming, when you consider that colour clients will normally need between 2 and 4 products to maintain their hair and style, and products in some areas of beauty treatment home care cost much more.

In addition to the "home care" range you need the ancillary items such as hair straighteners, hair dryers and gifts for other people.

The previous example is based on a very low single product price. More often or not your clients will require more than one product on each visit.

From experience I would be expecting all industry professionals to easily achieve £/$100.00 per stylist per day on retail products.

This is also possible in the barbering industry because client numbers are often greater than other parts of the Hair and Beauty sector.

This would now mean:

1 person (even if you are working on your own or renting a space) could generate £/S 500.00 per week, or £/S26,000 per year.

2 persons   =   £/S 52,000.00 per year

3 persons   =   £/S 78,000.00 per year

6 persons   =   £/S 156,000.00 per year

10 persons   =   £/S 260,000.00 per year

All with no extra staff and no extra time booked out, and you could do this today.

As the barbering sector is still the fastest growing part of the hair and beauty sector in 2019, this is what it means for you.

Barbershop. (Most shops service between 2 and 4 persons per hour.) Average product price £/S12.00

1 Full time Barber working 40 hours per week.

Average of 15 clients per day or 75 per week

40% of these gives you 30 clients x £/S12.00 = £/S 360.00 per week.

1 barber (even if you are working on your own or renting a space) could generate £/$ 360.00 per week, or £/$ 18,720.00 per year.

1 Barber	=	£/$ 18,720.00 per year
2 Barbers	=	£/$ 37,440.00 per year
3 Barbers	=	£/$ 56.160.00 per year
4 Barbers	=	£/$ 74,880.00 per year

If thousands of pounds of extra sales are not enough to convince you to make your life better, then perhaps **PROFIT** will.

The average net profit (that is left after you have paid everything) on a service is between 5 and 10 percent.

Therefore, a service costing £/$ 30.00 and taking an hour will leave you with a net profit of £/$1.50 to £/$ 3.00 on average in the UK/USA. Selling products is much more profitable.

A £/$ 10.00 gents haircut taking 30 minutes and leaves you with an average net profit of between 50p/c and £/$1 in the UK/USA. Selling products is much more profitable.

However, the average branded product from some of the leading industry suppliers, give a net profit of 40% and takes very little, or no extra time to sell it. During or after the service. There are no measurable wage costs involved.

Therefore, selling a £/$15.00 product would give you about £/$6.00 (after deductions for delivery, tax and salon use.) To me this feels like money for doing almost nothing at all.

OWN BRAND PROFITS
"YOUR OWN BRAND MUST BE THE PREMIUM BRAND."

But here is the deal maker for many of you: if you organise your own brand or develop a white label your net profit can be over 100% because you have more control over the retail price. You can quite easily make £/$10.00 per item with good buying practice. You should have two product ranges in your salon, per type of service. One of them should be your own brand, with your salon brand name on it. This product range needs to be the premium product. This means making it more expensive than the other product range that you have.

Whether you need great sales for cash flow or great profits for investment, you must now be convinced that products can do both for your business. Selling (retailing) could potentially represent over half of your sales depending on your salon service price point and deliver exceptional profits that you cannot walk away from.

> **CUSTOMER FOCUS**
>
> "THE NUMBER OF CLIENTS SOLD TO, IS MORE IMPORTANT THAN THE VALUE OF THE PRODUCTS SOLD."

When you are trying to increase salon sales through products, do not focus on the total financial target with the team member. You must focus on the percentage of clients that are successfully sold to. This focus drives customer service, which in turn drives the sales revenue. If you aim for the financial target first the team will focus on achieving the target with as few clients as possible, which avoids the long-term objective of product selling.

Is this important to you?

Whilst very few owners and stylists appear to agree that product selling is essential for a successful business, there are also very few people who disagree that customer service is perhaps the most important aspect of their business or their job. Everything you do is for the benefit of the client, so that they are happy and will return time and time again. We create beautiful salons and spas, furnish them with Italian furniture and serve better drinks than the Ritz hotel. We go to extra ordinary lengths to achieve colour perfection, massage rooms where the client is bathed in candle light and exotic oils. Our barbershops have machines providing fine coffee, boutique leather sofas and barber chairs costing as much as a small car. Everything that the client might want, but what about what they actually need?

Identifying what the customer needs is the most important part of customer service and product selling, therefore they are the same thing. To be successful in product sales you must disregard all the reasons that you have ever conjured up in your mind and dispose of any excuses people have ever passed onto you.

If they do, and they will almost always NEED something, you are now duty bound to find out what they NEED, help them realise what they NEED and SELL them the product. Think about it, how can a client NEED something because they have a problem, yet you choose not to help them solve that problem? That is not customer service, it is customer neglect.

WHAT DOES THE CLIENT NEED?

"FAILING TO SOLVE A CLIENTS PROBLEM IS NOT CUSTOMER SERVICE, IT IS CUSTOMER NEGLECT."

Selling something that they DO NOT NEED is also completely unacceptable. Neither you as an industry professional, or salon owner, will benefit.

Customer service and product selling is the same thing.

Carl Hinder/Sell products or die (not) trying

Imagine the following scenario: following a consultation a wonderful new client books in for a colour service, with a restyle and blow dry, you use your expertise and agree on the dual colours, she is quoted a hundred pounds/dollars and returns a few days later.

After spending a few hours with you, the client could not be more pleased with the new red tones as she sways her head from side to side in the mirror, flicking her head back as she watches her silky hair fall back into the perfect bob cut. She pays her bill and even leaves an enormous tip for her new stylist.

The customer leaves the salon looking and feeling amazing, and very happy with her salon experience. So far so good.

So great customer service: most salons would be very proud of their work and the exceptional customer service, she did leave a huge tip after all, you feel that you could not do anymore.

Two days later she decides that she needs to wash her hair, she takes a shower as normal and uses her normal shampoo which never lets her down, after all she has been using it for years. It always removes her dandruff, and now of course it will remove some of the fabulous new colour too. It is the first wash and a little colour runs out, that is normal of course.

Like most people she showers daily, a little colour runs each day, and after a week she finds herself at home stood in front of the mirror. She wonders to herself, where is that lovely colour that I had done last week? From the lovely salon with the lovely stylist and pretty much decides that they are not very lovely at all anymore. Now all she can think about is the wasted money and how awful she looks, what are her friends and colleagues are saying about her?

What an awful way to make a client feel.
She now feels disappointed and only because you did not take customer service to that next step.

Is this really any salons idea of customer service?

If you have not bought into why you must sell yet, you will now be collecting all the dozens of excuses that you have learnt, ready to defend yourself. This is not about you, it is CUSTOMER SERVICE not Stylist service.

> ## THINK ABOUT IT
>
> "IT IS CALLED CUSTOMER SERVICE, NOT STYLIST SERVICE."

Carl Hinder/Sell products or die (not) trying

This is an example of very poor service, and you both get to lose. It is not just your reputation as a stylist and a salon that has been damaged, but she probably will not come back and instead head to another salon or the dreaded box colour. (Supermarket wins again)

Not everyone has a colour of course.

Maybe you are a Barber shop owner or an employee at a blow dry bar. Let us look at this view: you use a product to help blow dry their hair (sometimes) maybe a thickening cream, a product to style and hold their hair, maybe a clay or wax and sometimes even set it with a hair spray. You use these products because YOU NEED them to create a finished style that you are proud of.

I do not believe that any Barber, Stylist or Therapist ever lets a client leave the salon, whilst thinking "I did a terrible job there". To the contrary, you are pedantic in every detail of the final creation, teasing every hair until it meets with perfection, or at least your version of perfection. You are proud of both your work and your reputation, and you know what leaves the salon is a reflection on you and the business. As the service is complete you dance around the mirror holding another hand-held mirror at a dozen different angles behind them, smiling and nodding until you get confirmation that their creation is awesome, and usually it is.

The client leaves knowing that they look amazing and you praise yourself as your walking advert struts down the street. Now isnt that great customer service?

No, it is not. It is not even good service.

Where is your pride and reputation a few days later?

If you need products in the salon to create that finished style today, then it should logically follow that the client will need the same products to create the same finished style tomorrow.

If the clients style does not need them to create that style tomorrow, then why are you using them today?

Of course, they need them, but clients leave too often without the products that they NEED.

THE CLIENT MUST NEED THEM

"IF YOU NEED TO USE THEM ON THE CLIENT TODAY, THEN IT LOGICALLY FOLLOWS THAT THE CLIENT WILL NEED THEM TOMORROW."

The client now must remedy this problem, the one that you created for them, by trying to find something that will work from someone else.

Maybe they go online and wait a few days for delivery, maybe they will go to the supermarket for advice and products, (can you hear how ridiculous that sounds) maybe they will pop into another salon or maybe they just go without and look awful for a couple of weeks. Even if they find a product, it is probably nothing like the one you would like them to use to recreate your master piece.

You, the salon owner, the stylist, the barber, the therapist could have prevented all this inconvenience and hassle by simply selling the client the correct products when they were in the salon. Your failure to sell, to meet the clients NEEDS has resulted in poor customer service. Delivering the best in-salon service is only half the job.

Important change. You need to change the way you think about customer service, and how long you spend with your clients. Think about owning your client from the moment they enter the salon until the moment they return to the salon, possibly weeks or months later. Take responsibility for how they look every day, not just the couple of hours that they are sat in your chair.

This means that not only must they leave the salon with the correct products that they NEED, but they also NEED the knowledge on how to apply them, which way to brush their hair, how to hold the hair dryer, which brush they NEED, you must educate them and look after them, even if that means phoning them in a few days and then again in a few weeks after their service and asking if they are managing their new style and do they still have enough product? If not drop it off to them, find a way of getting that product to them as soon as possible, do not let them go looking. They might find somewhere else that they prefer.

GIVE MORE

"IT IS NOT JUST ABOUT THE PRODUCT, IT IS ABOUT GIVING MORE. GIVE MORE ATTENTION, GIVE MORE TIME, GIVE MORE SERVICE."

It is important that you think of this as a people business, not the products business, which is why we call it customer service and not product service. It is all about the client, they should be at the centre of your attention, you must sell the client on the products not actually sell a product to the client. A client is sold on the product when they realise what it can do for them.

Carl Hinder/Sell products or die (not) trying

They do not buy the product because they want a product, they buy the product because it has features that they want, and because they know those features will make them feel good, and they know they need those benefits.

In summary you cannot deliver great customer service unless you sell a client on a product which they need, once they are sold on it, they will buy the item. The client NEEDS it. If you are a salon owner your staff must understand, that they are only doing half the job if they are not selling products. Ultimately, if they cannot understand the unbreakable connection between customer service and product selling you may need to start the search new staff.

But not until you have finished this book and put them through the online course.

TO RETAIN MORE CUSTOMERS

Is keeping your clients important to you?

It should be. It is much more expensive to recruit new clients than keeping your current ones, and you will find it almost impossible to grow your business without doing both.

There are some widely accepted figures in the industry that correlate product sales with retention/loyalty:

Customer buys 1 product — they are 30% more likely to return than if they bought none.

Customer buys 2 products — they are 60% more likely to return than if they bought none.

Customer buys 3 products — they are 90% more likely to return than if they bought none.

There are two very simple reasons why this is.

Firstly, a client who has a full service with you and then buys the products that they NEED have a stronger sense of relationship, they have bought into the whole deal. They have bought into you, your advice, your trust worthiness and your salon.

Secondly, the products have enabled the client to maintain their hair colour, skin condition, nail condition, their perfect tan or a fabulous hair style, meaning that they look and feel good every day.

They know that it was you who created this for them, and it is you they will want to come back to, not just as a client but as a raving fan of yours.

There really are no business reasons why you should not be selling products that customers NEED.

When 90% of your competitors do not sell products and do not deliver customer service through product sales, can you imagine how disappointed they will be if they ever leave you for another salon? I am sure a lot will be right back.

CUSTOMER RETENTION

"CLIENTS BUY FROM PEOPLE THEY TRUST, THE MORE THEY BUY THE MORE THEY TRUST YOU, THE MORE THEY TRUST YOU, THE MORE LOYAL THEY ARE."

BECAUSE IT IS GREAT MARKETING

Better than marketing, it is FREE marketing.

Having your clients going around with a bad hairstyle because they are using the wrong product, the colour has faded out from using the wrong shampoo, or a streaky tan from not using the right after lotion is a walking disaster for you. Emotionally you will never bond with the client because when the client looks in the mirror every morning, they are reminded of you in a negative way.

However, you can turn that around very easily, and as described earlier, not only can you create a raving fan from making them look and feel good every day between visits, but they are now a walking billboard for you. Not only will they be visually fantastic but when other people comment on how good they look, they will gush with pride and make you and your salon sound like a luxury holiday in Mauritius. These referrals are so powerful, people will act on them and you will see them in your shop pretty soon. If that is not enough for you, all this advertising is free, which means more clients, which means more sales.

I have genuinely seen women hurtling across a supermarket floor. Changing direction like a Cheetah chasing a Gazelle, with an alertness that comes from drinking too much coffee, to track down another woman who had passed them with an amazing color or cut. After the suspect has been apprehended, they discuss the various hair options like they had been friends for years, this is the point that can only ever be achieved with great service and great products.

Lots of spa and clinic treatments are private or unseen by anyone but the client. However, even here, the product part of the service is essential for all the reasons given, including the FREE marketing. One of our more personal therapies might be Colonic Hydrotherapy and something you might not think would be subject to the "word of mouth" marketing. But when combined with great therapy management and products such as nutritional supplements, the client will see the benefits are so large, that they will want to share them with friends, family and other health conscious people. Without the correct products or dietary information, the benefits are not maximised, and neither is the free marketing.

If a woman has a skin treatment at a spa, I am sure she will feel great, maybe for a day or so. Where she has bought the skin care package, she will invariably have longer term benefits than having the treatment alone.

Carl Hinder/Sell products or die (not) trying

She may well feel as if she looks much better, she may feel exuberant, toned or refreshed and it is these emotions that she will want to share and give you and your business free marketing.

This is not exclusive to women either, men will talk to each other at social gatherings and at work if they see a colleague or workmate with a stand out haircut, style, colour or beard trim. We may not show so much fervor as the ladies, but we are certainly aware.

I once stood in a long queue at a Costa coffee shop, it was about 7.30 in the morning and the place was full of people in business dress getting their caffeine kick before the office onslaught. About ten places in front of me was a tall, strong looking gentleman with a wide neck and greying hair. I was initially fixated on the back of his head and his neckline as if it were the most interesting work of art in an art gallery, combined with a level of boredom that comes from early morning queues. The style was short, very textured and defined, like a catalogue model, defined sides and the most precise square neck line up and neck shave (in the days when square necks were fashionable), like it had been drawn on using an architects ruler. I could not quite see the front until eventually the queue shuffled along and the big gent picked up his coffee and headed towards me.

My early morning brain engaged, "Hi Mike, how are you Sir" I spouted to him, I did not realise until the moment as he walked towards me, he was one of our salon clients. Even though I never discussed his cut with him that morning, I am sure I would have if he were a stranger.

When other people see this kind of standard, which in part is achieved by ensuring the client has the correct products and they are being used correctly, they will be impressed, the word will spread, and you get Free marketing.

The great thing about getting free marketing this way, is that it is an endless supply, all you must do is just keep repeating the process.

FREE MARKETING
"PRODUCTS MAKE YOUR FREE MARKETING LAST LONGER."

Own branded products are great for marketing.

Promote your own brand products above any other brands.

If you do not have your own brand alternative, now is the time to get one. This can sometimes be a little tricky in parts of the beauty sector, but it can be done, and you should do everything to achieve ranging your own products.

The own brand product must be the premium option.

When the client buys this they will take it home and put it in their bathroom, in their holiday bags, their business overnight bag and when you get really smart you will sell them products for their friends and family too, which will go into bathrooms and travel bags wide and far. Every day people go into their bathroom a minimum of twice a day, that is twice a day they get to see your item staring them in the face, perhaps even applied to their face. A shampoo, a body wash, a conditioner, a skin lotion, a colour restorer, a massage oil, a beard oil, depilatory cream the list is lengthy. All these wonderful products that the client NEEDS are advertising your work and your business every day and for FREE. Why would you want to promote some other company if you have choice?

This free marketing comes with one important stipulation of course, and that is the product must be the right one for the client and they must need it. Otherwise the client is reminded every day of the bad decision that they made.

TO REDUCE YOUR VALUE ADDED TAX (VAT) — UK MAINLY

Even though this is a UK based tax there are sales taxes all over the world that are similar.

VAT is one of the top five messages or calls that I get every week. Salon owners panicking that the accountant has just told them that they went over the limit two months ago, or they will shortly be hitting the threshold any moment. It is almost as if the threshold for this tax is invisible to salon owners until the last minute. Salon owners creep towards the threshold every week and take no action at all to deal with it.

What is the big deal? Why are salons so concerned? Well once you hit the threshold for VAT you must collect (give) a percentage of your sales to the Government, currently 20% in the UK. The current UK threshold is £85,000. There are other flat rate schemes with a lower percentage available, but they are only temporary and of course legislation can change at any time.

This registration process and payment can mean having to give 20%, a fifth of your turnover to the government, in a change that can happen in one day. This means you feel as if you are 20% worse off than yesterday, and in this scenario you pretty much are.

Just to stay the same in terms of sales you must jump from £85,000 to £106,000 in one day! This of course is impossible, unless you are opening another salon or redeveloping your property.

Far too many salons spend an inordinate amount of time and energy avoiding the VAT threshold, and perhaps if you are a one-person operation, it might be a viable option. For serious business owners looking to have financial freedom, you should embrace it and manage it. Think of it this way, the more tax you pay the more successful you must be. Avoiding it either means trading down or trying to conjure up some semi legal scheme to avoid it, neither are an option if you want to be highly successful, or indeed stay out of prison.

You truly need to make VAT just part of business life and something not to be feared. The key to overcoming VAT and indeed managing all costs is sales. Salons make a huge mistake in trying to grow organically, slowly, steadily, trying to manage the risk of failure. In reality you are nearer to failure by doing it this way than accelerating the process.

If you are a serious salon owner then you are going to be at the VAT threshold in a few months, maybe a year. If you are focused on generating financial wealth you need to register for VAT from day one.

This enables you to manage prices better for your clients and if you have a lot of property development costs when setting the business up you will be able to reclaim these too.

For many salons a price increase will really help manage the new tax liability, this must be considered, and in most cases implemented. When you start your business, you should build the VAT rate into your pricing structure from day one, you will very soon be over the VAT level anyway.

> ## EMBRACE VAT
> "IF YOU ARE SERIOUS ABOUT FINANCIAL SUCCESS, VAT MUST BE MANAGED. SELLING PRODUCTS IS AN EFFECTIVE WAY OF DOING THIS."

The product selling or retail offer.

I rarely use the words "retail offer" even though it is widely used throughout most retail business. This to me, implies that there is an option, an 'offer' which you can either accept or refuse, an offer that I can either present or withdraw. Selling on the other hand infers that there is only one right option, and that is the one the client should buy.

A great product selling commitment, alongside a price increase will remove most of your VAT stresses, especially if you are a transitioning salon from Non-VAT to VAT.

If you are already registered this is going to put an enormous amount of money into your till and into your bottom line.

E.g. One product.

A typical £15 product will cost around £9 for the salon to purchase.

You will pay £1.80 vat on. You can claim back this VAT from Customs and Excise.

You then sell it for £15.00. £3.00 of this is collected VAT. This means that you take the £3.00 collected and claim back what you have paid when you bought the product.

£3.00 collected minus the £1.80 already paid equals **£1.20 which you send to the tax man.**

A service (without products)

If this was a £15.00 service, you would pay £3.00 VAT to the tax man.

On a product costing £15.00 you would only pay £1.20.

Saving £1.80 every time.

On a £150.00 service you would pay £30.00 VAT to the tax man.

On £150.00 worth of products you would only pay £12.00 VAT.

Saving £18.00 every time.

When you couple this with the fact that you can now claim back VAT on all your bills that you have not been able to since you opened, such as utilities, sundries, stock etc. then the VAT impact becomes relatively small.

Product sales are fantastic for helping you manage your VAT bill.

Carl Hinder/Sell products or die (not) trying

PART 3: WHY YOU DO NOT SELL

Carl Hinder/Sell products or die (not) trying

THE MYTHS AND THE EXCUSES

Whenever I have a discussion with a salon, barbershop, spa, clinic, or run a training course on this subject there are always a list of objections and excuses. Most of them learned responses from others in our industry, and it is only the Hair & Beauty industry that suffer with this.

I have worked with a lot of different types of business over the years and you never come across a waiter refusing to sell you the wine, to complement your food, or only asking you what you would like for main course but not asking about desert. Of course not, because it is part of their training, culture, job expectation and if nothing else because their boss would never allow it. The boss knows that the business would never survive, and the client by and large would be unhappy with the overall service. There are number excuses that I am presented with on a regular basis. I never allow them to be accepted and neither should you, they are not reasons, they are barriers which largely do not exist. People with excuses have no sales targets that they are held to, and they are not trying to build their column or client base.

Before we take down the barriers, let me tell you the main and possibly the only reason that salons and staff fail to sell products. It is because the staff and often the owners do not want to be told NO, by the client. No, feels like rejection, and most human beings do not accept rejection too well, it is part of what makes us human. Currently, the fear of what feels like rejection is greater than the feeling of reward, when they get the selling process right.

Because of this worry of rejection the stylist positions themselves in the path of least resistance, sometimes unknowingly, other times deliberately. The sooner they can find their reason for not selling the sooner they feel better about themselves. Sometimes they will be so good at it that they will find the reason before the client even sets foot in the salon.

They are the masters of the selling avoidance technique.

These avoidance techniques which you must eradicate are:

I AM NOT A SALES PERSON AND IT IS NOT MY JOB

No matter how you look at your role as a salon owner or a stylist, you are a sales person, and selling is what you do. Selling a lot will result in success and selling too little will result in failure. We have already covered this in the previous sections, but it is worth reviewing again because this excuse is usually the first line of attempted escape. We have already established that everyone is a sales person whether they are trying or not, quite obviously some are better at it than others and some will need more training than others. We also established that it is almost impossible to deliver total customer service without selling products, and if customer service is part of your job then product selling also must be part of the same job.

From a wider perspective as a salon owner your job is nothing but to sell, not just products but yourself, your business, your ideas, your ethos and not just to your team but often your family, your friends and certainly the public. You might be a hair stylist, therapist or barber as well as the owner, but you are first and foremost a salesperson. Can you think of any super successful business that the owner is not a salesperson above all else?

Carl Hinder/Sell products or die (not) trying

Sir Richard Branson, Sir Alan Sugar, Mark Zuckerberg, even the Kardashian family do nothing but sell. If you want a successful business, you and all your team must learn to sell. You can do it and it is your job to do it.

Around 70% of salon clients are never even asked if they would like a salon product to purchase. If you do not ask them, what can they do but look elsewhere?

Imagine how impressed they are when they change salons and are presented with the right items for them. They are not coming back to you for sure.

About fifteen years ago we had a great salon business and a premium account with a colour house. We bought so much stock directly from them that I saw the area manager more often than some of my friends. We were always looking for new ideas and that often meant visiting other salons and meeting the owners for a salon walk around and lunch.
We decided to visit a salon around twenty miles from one of my salons in a small but what I would call a middle-class market town. This part of the town only had two salons, and the one we had arranged to visit was clearly the best presented of the two. I had been told that the salon owner was very business focused and her salon image re-enforced that view too.

Carl Hinder/Sell products or die (not) trying

At the front of the salon was a large reception desk framed with two huge product stands, and two opposing walls lined with large mirrors and great lighting.

Following the introductions and the salon tour, I wandered around chatting with some of the smartly dressed staff, and some of the clients. They were all pretty busy, so the salon manager, the area manager and I decided to head out for a short working lunch.
The owner got the attention of the receptionist as were leaving and said a few good byes to the clients just finishing their services, especially the ones at the reception desk. After quickly checking out the competition, by standing in their shop windows and nodding at each other like judges off a reality TV show we decided that grabbing a sandwich and heading back to the salon would be a great idea.

We found what I would describe as a boutique supermarket, like a farm shop, but with a lot more than just fresh food. We selected some vittles and shuffled towards the checkout. In front of us was a client from the salon, one that I had spoken to earlier, and she and the salon owner again engaged in polite conversation. When it was her turn the salon client heaved a hand basket full of items onto the checkout belt.

When I say items I mainly mean, Shampoo, Conditioner, Hair Spray and other toiletry style products. The three of us looked at each other in turn, like we were communicating using telepathy and raised eye brows. The area manager took the initiative and asked the lady "were you not just in the hair salon? She said "yes, I saw you all in there." The area manager went on, "may I ask you why you did not get those products when you were in the salon?" We all waited with bated breath, like were waiting for our lottery numbers to come up, the moment of declaration,

"I did not know you sold them" she said.

On our return to the salon we shared our discovery with the stylist that had spent a couple of hours with her earlier that day to find out how someone could be in the salon so long and not even know that we sell what she needs. The stylist, quite genuinely and without any emotion, simply told us that she thought that selling products was not really her job unless the client asked her for something. Instead, she preferred to just look after the clients hair. This was the stylist way of avoiding rejection and making herself feel better, she had no interest in delivering great customer service.

Carl Hinder/Sell products or die (not) trying

If you are a stylist and you really think that not selling is okay, you need to review your understanding of customer service and business.

You have a duty to make the salon owner, which could be you, as much money as possible, and make the client as happy as possible. You cannot do either if you are not selling products.

Unless everyone in the business sells there will not be enough cash to invest the future.

A salon cannot offer pay rises, staff training, staff incentives, receptionists, salon trainers, salon managers or to invest in new equipment. Business expansion, promotion and everything else depends on you realising that your job is to sell.

If you are a salon owner and your team actually think they are not sales people you are not training them properly, or managing them with sales targets, and if you are not managing them with sales targets, you are not really managing them at all.

It is every ones duty to sell.

Carl Hinder/Sell products or die (not) trying

THE PRODUCTS ARE TOO EXPENSIVE TO SELL

Nothing is ever too expensive in the salon. Everybody that visits your salon has the money to spend on products that they need. However, they may not choose to give you their money in return for a product for three reasons:

1) They are unsure and afraid to make a mistake buying the wrong product, especially if they are used to something else.

2) They do not think there is enough value in the exchange. The client has to be convinced that by handing over this money they will get a certain amount of benefit from the product. If the level of benefit seems too low, then they do not want to do the exchange.

3) They sense that you are not sold on the product, if you are not convinced neither will they be.

Let us take number one. The more buying mistakes a client makes the more they want to get right in the future, and not buying anything can sometimes be safer than taking the risk. We have all made mistakes when buying something in the past, a second-hand car that broke down after 3 months, a pair of shoes that you hardly ever wore and are now sitting in the bottom of your wardrobe, a holiday that was just not what you thought it would be.

Well everyone has these experiences and they become ingrained in us.

The more mistakes we make the harder we try to not make them. At a conscious level, I am sure most people do not even realise that they are doing it, and use other verbal excuses, like price. But that is not the real reason.

Not many clients will tell you that price is the problem, normally the stylist makes that decision for them, but even if the client does say it is price, it is almost certainly not. You should ignore it. At this stage it is just a barrier that you are happy to accept so that you do not have to go through the selling process and possibly get rejected. The sooner you find the excuse the sooner you feel relieved, that the process is over.

This means that you are the problem, not the client and not the price.

Number two. The reason the client NEEDS a product is because they have a problem which needs a solution. You must help them find the solution. If you convince the client that you can do more than solve their problem, they will buy it from you regardless of the price. Imagine that a client has dandruff, you would be a very poor professional if you did not identify and discuss this with the client. Once the problem is identified the client will want a solution.

That solution might be in part a dandruff shampoo, which you will of course explain to the client. This is not the end of the process, maybe this is not enough value for them, may be that is not enough benefit. It is not always what you say that is the problem, it is what you do not say, what you have left out can be more important than what you have so far put in.

Now take this up a notch, explain to the customer that the dandruff maybe a result of their working environment, medication, diet or stress, this expertise now gets them buying into you, you are selling yourself. Explain that reducing the dandruff means that they will not have any "snow" on their clothes, perhaps they can wear their hair differently and that perhaps the shampoo will help them if they have oily hair too. It is these kinds of benefits that will register with the client and get you closer to your sale.

They may still say price is an issue, and that means the value or the benefit to them is still not big enough, or it could be that the customer is just lying to you or there is another reason. Do not give up though, customers lie to you all the time, they lie when they cancel a booking, they lie when they tell you the length of their hair over the phone, they even lie to you when they have a supermarket colour on and deny it. Not all of them, and not all the time, but it is a factor which you should keep to yourself and in the back of your mind.

Number three. They sense that you are not sold on the product. Nobody buys anything from someone that does not sound convincing. When someone tells you something with passion, energy and determination you will believe them, even if they are not telling the truth. Sometimes these people are so bought into their own words, you might even know that they are lying, but their passion affects you, and you now want to believe them, you will even tell yourself to give them the benefit of the doubt. I am not for one moment suggesting that you tell lies or mislead a client in any way, but you must establish the truth and convey the information with passion and commitment.

If you do not believe in the product, if you are not sold on the price the client will know and they will doubt their ability to make the right decision. They will know that you think the products are too expensive and adopt your position. The price is not stopping this sale, your lack of commitment to the product is. It is you stopping the sale, not the client rejecting it.

One of the most obvious things that should be pointed out to the price sensitive client is the great value that they get from a product. Highlight it to them like this. Let us use a mens haircut for simplicity, but this is true of almost every service in the industry, with a few exceptions.

Carl Hinder/Sell products or die (not) trying

The gentlemans haircut costs £/$15 in some places, and the products around £/$15 too. The haircut will last about 4 weeks, often a lot less. The product will last three months. If the client is looking for value and most are, then showing that the product last three to six times as long as his haircut for the same price is very powerful. That, and the fact that he needs it to keep him looking amazing.

If you still think its price, and it really is not! Take this salon challenge: pick a product and reduce the price by 25%, so just above cost. Write down what you sold last month of this item, then in three months time, have a look what you sold in that third month. I almost guarantee it will be exactly the same. Price is not a major factor in selling salon products. You are the major factor in selling salon products.

Remember, clients can compare how your shop looks, or how your prices compare, but they cannot compare the salon experience over the internet, make your business about experience and customer service and your competition will diminish.

Carl Hinder/Sell products or die (not) trying

THE CLIENT DOES NOT HAVE ENOUGH MONEY

Most stylists decide this without even finding out if it is really true, they decide for themselves, sometimes they even decide before the client arrives in the salon. Sometimes it is because the client is a regular and you have formed an opinion based on the stories of their life that they tell you. But because you do not want to help them by selling them things that they NEED, you sub consciously gather all the things that support your theory. She is on a pension, he has lost his job, she lives on her own, his wife left him with three children, she has just recovered from a terrible illness, someone broke into her house and stole all her jewelry etc. Offer a little sympathy for sure, but you were not listening to what was really going on. Why would you really listen when you had found your barrier and you are not going to let anyone take it away from you.

You are reading this now thinking he is wrong, he is wrong about price, he is wrong about everything, what I am right about is that these are just barriers.

You are in charge of your own emotions and actions, how the client feels about the transaction is not your fault. If a client is genuinely upset, objecting emotionally, ask yourself this; are they upset with you or themselves?

If a client genuinely has no money for a product, is that your fault or their fault. If they have no money it is their fault of course, one way or another they have failed to generate enough income, their income is not your responsibility. Your income is your responsibility.

The point is, even though they may genuinely not have enough money, which is very rare, you do not need to feel bad, you do not need to make excuses for them or feel as if you are being pushy. You still need to educate the client to the expected standard. If a client can afford a £/$75 colour service, then they cannot afford to be without the shampoo that looks after it. How can someone not afford a £/$15 colour shampoo but afford to destroy their £/$75 colour within a week? It is not logical.

I have never heard a customer actually use those words

"I do not have enough money," they might not have enough money on them at that moment in time, but sure they have enough money for things they need and sometimes just want. We all do. Try, "that is not a problem Madam, we accept Visa and Mastercard."

How many people, probably including you, go and book a holiday with a set budget. Right, I can only afford £/$ 500.00 for a one-week holiday in Spain, and off you go to book it, online or at the travel agents.

However, when you go to actually book it you discover that for just £/$100 more you can have an 'all inclusive' deal for your food and drink, immediately you consider how much money that could save you. You are considering spending more to save money.

For another £/$50 you can have a room with a balcony overlooking the ocean to watch the sunset, wow, you are sure that would be just amazing. The thought process begins, 'I will book that instead, I have worked hard this year, had some tough times, I can just cut back on my nights out for a few weeks and I can put the rest on my credit card'.

You can spend 30% more on your holiday because someone (maybe yourself) convinced you that the value of the holiday was more important than the money. You felt you had greater benefit by spending more. Your clients are exactly the same.

VALUE OVERRIDES PRICE

"WHEN THE VALUE OF A PRODUCT IS MORE IMPORTANT THAN OWNING THE CASH, PRICE WILL NOT BE IMPORTANT."

Carl Hinder/Sell products or die (not) trying

A few years ago, I was in one of my salons just working with the team, clients coming and going and just coaching the team really. The salon manager, with an excellent selling record had just completed a full colour service on a female client, who was of retirement age. The manager escorted her to the reception desk, gathered her belongings and took payment. I held the door open for the client, thanking her for her custom and walked back over to the desk. It was a small desk that sat just in front of a very large double aspect window, the manager was still lingering there so I asked,
 "how come we did not sell her any products?", she replied,
 "oh she is retired bless her, she has not got much money".

I hardly had time to launch into a response about how retired people were now the most affluent sector in general society, with good pensions and savings (this was before the 2008 financial crash, but it is still widely true today), when like a slow motion drive by gangster movie the client drove past the window, with a smile and a nodding motion that projected "I got you guys this time," as we admired her brand new, silver, C class Mercedes Benz. There was not a lot more to say that day.

This point is not about whether pensioners or anyone else can afford the item, it is about you not deciding on their behalf whether they can or not, and even then, they may not be telling you the truth.

THEY CAN GET IT CHEAPER ON THE INTERNET

This has become the new escape route for stylists over the past few years. Certainly, if you had two identical branded products you could find somewhere on the internet that is slightly cheaper. But we have just established that price is not the reason that people do not buy from you, you are the reason why people either buy from you or not. People enjoy convenience as much as anything, and whilst the internet can be convenient there is nothing quicker and easier than going home with the correct product there and then, knowing how to use it properly and being able to use it that day, not even the internet can compete with that.

I have heard anecdotal tales of clients going home to buy a product on the internet for £/$1 less than in your salon. This may be true, but it was not the lower price that made them do this, it is more likely that there was something you missed in educating your client or something missing in your relationship that made them do this.

If these tales are true (and they are not) then lower your prices by a £/$1, what are you waiting for? If they shop online because they get reward points, give them reward points. If they want free quick delivery, well it will not get much quicker or freer than buying it there and then.

If they want a product in between salon visits set up a web page and post it to them or drop it in their home on the way home. You must not accept any of the psychological barriers that are damaging your business.

If you have still not bought into what I am saying about the internet let me give you a 100% full proof way of beating it. By now you should have done what I told you to do earlier in the book and set up you own brand. For some business like hair salons and barber shops this is one phone call away, very easy to achieve. For the beauty, spa and clinic sector you will have a bit more work to do but do it you must. Even if, like me you do not think that the internet is having a big effect on salon product sales, the own branded ones still give you Kudos over the competition, a huge profit margin and free marketing. If you have a shampoo, hair wax, skin regeneration cream or just about any product and promote it in the salon, the public will learn that they can only get this item from you or your own website. End of internet distraction.

It's all about you changing, it is about you becoming fully educated on how product selling can change your business life. Product sales are not complimentary, or an add-on of the service. Do not think like that, when you think it complements the service, you think that it is optional.

It is not optional, you cannot have great service without using a great product. They are the same thing. It is like buying a motor car, you must put oil in the engine, or the car will not work the next day.

> # IT IS NOT AN OPTION
> "WHEN YOU THINK THAT PRODUCT SELLING IS AN OPTION, YOU WILL NOT SELL ANYTHING."

It is not the clients fault that they are using the internet for a cheaper product, it is your fault that they are using the internet for a cheaper product.

I recently bought a Cannon camera for my online videos, for my vlogs. I had never owned a mirror less camera before and I did not really know if it was the right one for me, despite having looked at many online reviews. I needed some professional help and went to the market leading high street store. With the cash in my pocket (well credit card ready) I was certain that I would walk out of this shop with my new camera, ready to improve my online content. The assistant showed me the box, and after a bit of persuasion he took it out of the box and finally handed it to me, cautiously, as if I were going to run out of the shop. I guess that is always a risk with high value items on some high streets.

We discussed all the features that I had read about and how they should work, after some time he reclaimed the camera, prising it from me in a gentle but determined way. I did not feel too comfortable about this purchase now, I was not sure I was making the right decision after all, I did not know if this camera had the right features and benefits for me.

I now own that camera, I went home watched lots more Youtube videos and then bought it online, and yes, a little cheaper. It was not my fault that I did this, it was the salesmans fault. He made me leave the store without the item. If he had been more focused on the sale than he was on the security he would have turned the camera on, showed me how easy it was to use the flip up LCD screen, how the auto controls made it perfect for me, how easy it was to switch from video to still mode and so on. I would have been sold on the product, I would have been sold on him, I would have bought the item there and then and I would have paid the extra £/$100 for his advice and because our relationship would have made me feel assured about my decision.

TAKE RESPONSIBILITY

"IT IS NOT THE CLIENTS FAULT THAT THEY ARE USING THE INTERNET, IT IS YOUR FAULT."

THE CLIENT DOES NOT LIKE ME BEING TOO PUSHY

> **DO NOT PUSH ME**
>
> "HOW YOU FEEL ABOUT A TRANSACTION IS NOT AS IMPORTANT AS HOW THE CLIENT FEELS ABOUT THE TRANSACTION."

Your feelings and emotions should not get in the way of getting the client what they NEED. You are the professional, how you manage your emotions is up to you. If you cannot sell products then you cannot deliver customer service, if you cannot deliver customer service in our industry then you need to either work out how to do it (read this book and take the course) or look for an industry that does not need any customer service.

You are the one in control of any transaction, you are the one who can deliver the service. The client cannot deliver customer service, you deliver the customer service.

As Arkwright said in the British Sitcom about a corner shop — referring to the customers " what they come in for is up to them, what they go out with is up to us!"

TAKE CONTROL

"WHAT THE CLIENT COMES IN FOR IS UP TO THEM, WHAT THEY GO OUT WITH IS UP TO YOU."

The problem with the pushy argument is that you do not actually know what pushy is. You use the word pushy for any suggestion that you might make, and the client then disagrees with. Just because they disagreed with you does not mean you were being pushy. You take the clients product rejection as personal rejection; therefore, you think that was an indication that you were pushy.

Many stylists think they are being pushy even when they simply imagine in their minds that the client will disagree. Educating and Recommending something that the client NEEDS is not pushy.

Pushy

Adjective Word forms: ′**pushier** *or* ′**pushiest**
Informal
annoyingly aggressive and persistent

Webster′s New World College Dictionary, 4th Edition.

Carl Hinder/Sell products or die (not) trying

Based on this description, I can honestly say that I have never, ever met or seen a pushy stylist. I am not convinced that one exists.

Most people in our industry declare that the quality of being a pushy salesperson or stylist is a horrendous attribute to have, and if someone were aggressively selling, I would have to agree. However, passive pushy is everywhere we go, and we all accept it as normal.

Let us take an example:

When you visit a McDonalds fast food restaurant and most people have, try and order one single item, maybe a burger. Watch what happens.

"Is that a single or a double?"	— Single please
"Do want fries with that?"	— No thank you
"Large fries or regular fries"	— None thank you
"Would you like that as a meal deal "	— No thank you
"What drink would you like with that"	— None thankyou

You wait ten minutes and then you pick up your Big Mac meal, with large fries and a drink and head on over to your table, whatever happened to that simple burger? A whole pile of food that you never wanted, and you certainly do not need. You gave them all the no answers, well at least in your head you did but kept saying yes to the next up sell.

Now that is pushy, pushier than I have ever seen a stylist sell.

Would you keep asking more sales questions to a client? If they have already told you no to the first product. Well you should. If you genuinely believe the client needs an item, and you have been told no, you definitely keep going. Do not keep repeating the same question or benefit, find the piece of information that the client is looking for, the piece of information that will make them say yes.

The McDonalds system is so pushy that you get upset and decide to never go back ever again.

So pushy in fact that you did not even notice that you were buying a pile of food that you never needed or wanted, and so pushy that you were stood back at that counter a few weeks later.

      The point is you can be pushy, sometimes so pushy that clients do not even notice. With the added bonus, in our industry and in our salons the clients NEED what we are selling. You should never be afraid to sell something that the client needs. So, do not be afraid, you are not a second-hand car sales person selling dodgy motors that will break down in a week, you are selling fantastic super professional products that our clients need.

Trust me, no client ever gets home with fantastic products that work and they NEED and then feels as if you were too pushy.

> ## BEING PUSHY
> "THE FEAR OF BEING PUSHY IS ALL IN YOUR MIND, IT RARELY, IF EVER EXISTS IN YOUR SALON."

The negativity is all in your mind, you are doing these clients a favor, how else can they stay looking fantastic?

Of course, some people in some industries can be pushy, but just telling people things they need to know is not being pushy. We will discuss sales techniques to avoid pushing your clients away, but at the moment you are in no danger of doing that.

The first step is to stop worrying about how it makes you feel, and instead worry about how the client feels every time they go home empty handed. How do they feel, when they look in the mirror and wonder where their soft skin went, or why that awesome cut that they had a few days ago now looks like a Donald Trump special? What you should be feeling is disappointment with yourself, annoyed with yourself, frustrated with yourself for letting your client down.

Hopefully you are disappointed with yourself.

> ## BE DISAPPOINTED
> "DO NOT PRIDE YOURSELF ON NOT BEING PUSHY, BE DISAPPOINTED WITH YOURSELF FOR LETTING THE CLIENT DOWN WHEN THEY GO HOME EMPTY HANDED."

If you are, then now is the time to work out how to stop that happening, how to stop that feeling of failure. In the long run you and the client are both looking for the same thing, you both want a great experience and you both want to feel happy, and in most instances, you cannot do that without product advice and sales.

I have heard some people refer to this (pushy) as the "hard sell". First of all, get a grip on yourself! You are selling a bottle of shampoo, or face cream not a mansion house in Mayfair, London. Its £/$15, nobody is risking their families inheritance by buying a product that they need.

To avoid the "pushy" situation being mis-interpreted there are a few things that you can do to help. Do not keep repeating yourself with the same information, about the same product, at best you sound like you are nagging, at worse you sound like you have not a clue about the product.

Carl Hinder/Sell products or die (not) trying

Vary the information that the client might be looking for until they respond to something. Once they have responded or answered you do not repeat yourself again.

Think about what you are saying, limit your directional words like "you should get this" or "you must use this everyday", and mix them, or better replace them with "this will make you look amazing". Too much direction sounds as if you are in a rush to get the answer.

Do not confuse the pushy or hard sell excuse with what you really are, you are "passionate", and if you are passionate about a product the client will sense it and will whole heartedly take on board your advice. If you believe in yourself and your product, stick with it until the client goes home with it. If you do not believe in yourself or the product then that is where the problem is. Either you will give up, use the wrong words to educate the client or not try at all.

Be passionate.

Being consistent with customer service is not being pushy. There is a lot of market research information that says that a client needs to build up a picture before they make a purchase. How much time and how many contacts are dependent on the price, product complexity and of course the benefits to the client.

This means that they will need repeated information, unless they are extremely familiar with the salon or organisation and trust has already been built. So, while you are worrying about being pushy, you could well be just helping them gather information for a future purchase. I have seen figures of up to seven hours of combined marketing before the client acts. Probably a lot less in our industry, but whatever the actual figure, it is certainly true that clients do not often make impulse purchases and they like to build up their knowledge and confidence before making the purchase. You need to keep feeding the client with the benefits that they are looking for.

Finally, do not ever disagree with the client, even if they are wrong. This will close the conversation down completely.

ALWAYS AGREE

"NEVER, EVER DISAGREE WITH THE CLIENT, EVEN IF THEY ARE WRONG. DISAGREEING BRINGS YOUR CHANCE TO SELL TO AN END."

I HAVE NEVER BEEN ASKED TO SELL

Sadly, that is too often the truth.

The education system hardly touches the subject in relation to how important it is to sell products for the right reasons, the focus is on the softly, softly approach when it should be on the how to make money in business approach. I was recently at a college in the UK and I discussed this with the lecturer, he told me that whilst he did believe in product selling, he did not enforce it in the college, mainly because the profit from the product sale went back into the college funds and not into the students pockets. It seemed to me a bit churlish, when many of the students are subsidised by the government or the tax payer in the first place, and like everything else, the lower the funds available the lower the re-investment. This was a political angle that I was not especially keen to explore, but it was highly concerning from a different perspective. The attitude of this lecturer was born out of some misplaced loyalty, but the effect if his abstinence was bound to be much greater. When the lecturer only delivers minimal training in this area and has no expectation that the students should learn the importance and techniques of selling, the subsequent effect means that the students are never trained to accept selling as their duty.

Their clients (even in college) get to have poor service, their future salon clients get poor service and the salon owners get poor service. All this reduced service results in vastly reduced levels of sales and profits. I just do not see any winners here.

I have worked with a lot of colleges and training providers and the commitment to product selling is met with pretty much the same apathy.

Stylists, Barbers, therapists, technicians, cosmetologists the whole industry are focused on the creative mechanics of the service, the cut, the colour the massage, but they do not educate you on real customer service and they certainly do not educate you on how to make money and how to sell. The lack of ability to sell means salons fail to make much money, often they fail altogether. The industry is consumed by low wages and high staff turnover as great staff leave the industry.

Your boss never asked you to sell because they were all caught up with the myths and fear of selling themselves, and most still are. They know they should sell, but they could not do it when they were juniors, they could not do it when they were stylists and technicians and they cannot bear to get you to do it now they are the boss.

Carl Hinder/Sell products or die (not) trying

Even though they have a financial responsibility to themselves, their family and their team, selling remains taboo in their minds.

On occasion a brave salon owner will ask the team to start selling, the team often agree that it is the right thing to do, then go back to the sales floor and after a few hours go back to barely selling anything again. That is not asking to sell products, that is just asking the team to agree with you, which they do. Next time you ask (hopefully today) put the structures in place that mean that you keep asking and they keep selling.

You have now been asked to sell. I am asking you, please sell.

I DO NOT KNOW ANYTHING ABOUT THE PRODUCTS

Sadly, this is also true. But the lack of knowledge is a choice that you have personally made, whatever your position in the industry. Everyone should have the basic concept that a skin moisturiser goes on your skin, a tan enhancer goes on when you are using the sunbeds, a colour shampoo is for when you have just had colour and a dandruff shampoo is best used when someone has dandruff. As they say, that part is not rocket science. However, that level of product knowledge is not going to get you anywhere at all, or worse still it is not going to get your client what they need.

I have heard people in life saying, "I already know what I want," which as a business goal or life ambition is great, but if your salon customers are telling you that, it is not true. They may have had good experiences in other salons, although obviously not that good as they would not be sat in your chair today in your salon, and they may have picked up a bit of knowledge from them or from the internet. They cannot possibly be experts in our industry, they cannot know what they want because they do not know what is available, they do not know what it does for them, and they do not know how to use it.

Carl Hinder/Sell products or die (not) trying

You are, or should be the expert with all the knowledge and all the answers.

For years I would want the next piece of business software that would make me more efficient, get me ahead of my competition and even just make my life better. I spent hours online watching Youtube reviews, looking at the best deals, getting other peoples opinions until I clicked the buy button. Sometimes I was lucky, I got something that worked properly, more often or not the marketing was better than the product and I ended up buying some basic software that just did not do the job. I do not do that anymore, I either see a product that I think will change my world or I find a problem in my business that I need resolving, I have a quick look online then I phone my expert. Luckily, I have built up a great relationship with a software guru, at least that is what I call him. I tell him, "Simon I think I need this to resolve this problem," he tells me what will actually work and how much it costs, sends me the link and I am immediately in action with the thing that really works. He sells me what I need, using his knowledge.

It is exactly the same in your salon, your client has a problem, you are the guru, give them advice, they will take the advice and you make a sale. But, like Simon, you have to be top of your game, immersed in the product knowledge and then share it.

Nobody comes along and gives this product knowledge to Simon, he researches it, he takes responsibility for his own learning, how else can he be an expert? So, do not just wait for the product knowledge to come to you, go and get it now.

People cannot buy from you if they do not know about the product they are buying. If a client asks you a question, they want reassurance that you are an expert, that you know what this product will do and that you endorse it. If you waffle through educating your client, they will not trust you or the product. If they get home and the product does not do what you told them it will, the client will not trust the product, you or the salon again.

TAKE RESPONSIBILITY

"PRODUCT KNOWLEDGE IS YOUR PERSONAL RESPONSIBILITY, IT IS THE FOUNDATION OF ALL SALES."

Imagine going to buy a car from a show room: just like your salon the showroom is a lovely place with lovely smiling staff. You have money in your pocket, and you are ready to spend, just like your clients.

You know the car that you want, at least you think you do, but there are still things that are important to you and you need answers to be able to make a decision.

You commute to work every day, usually in wet weather conditions, you have two children and a caravan for weekends. It has to be the correct car for you,

So, you ask the salesperson "how many miles per gallon does this car do?" The sales person says that they are not sure but thinks it is about thirty or forty mpg, maybe more, maybe less.

You ask, "Are these tyres good in the rain?" The sales person says "yes of course, all new tyres are good in the rain, arent they?"

You ask, "Do these rear seats have anchor points for child seats?" The sales person says, "I guess they must have these days, they have seat belts"

You ask "Will I be able to tow a caravan with this car? Is it easy to fit a towing hitch?" The sales person says "Yes the engine has tons or torque, I have never seen a towing hitch fitted but I cannot see why not"

Are you feeling totally comfortable about parting with your £/$ 10,000 at the moment?

You do not know what the mileage (mpg) is like and how much it might cost you to get to work, you do not know if it is safe in the rain, you do not know if you can carry your small children and what on earth is torque? (at least the sales person was not pushy).

For me there would be no sale, I need to know how this product benefits me and after half an hour with the sales person I have not got a clue. If you want to sell your products, if you want to give fantastic customer service you need great salon product knowledge.

Product knowledge gives you credibility.

PRODUCT KNOWLEDGE
"PRODUCT KNOWLEDGE GIVES YOU CREDIBILITY WITH THE CLIENT."

WE HAVE NOT GOT EVERYTHING WE NEED

You of course do not need every item under the sun to be a good product seller (retailer), but you do need solutions for the problems that clients might have. Fortunately, the problems that clients usually have are very similar. You will solve 80% of your clients problems with 20% of the products range. This is known as Pareto's Principle. Pareto, an Italian economist used his mathematical formula to show how 20% of the people owned 80% of the wealth, what he did not perhaps realise is that it also forms the basis of many business principles, including 80% of your sales come from 20% of your products.

We normally call this the 80 — 20 rule.

This is great for you, as keeping 20% of items in stock at all costs will still return you 80% of your sales, in modern retailing we call these the HERO lines.

If you have taken my advice so far you will have two ranges of products in your salon. Hopefully one commercially branded and one salon branded. The chances of them both selling out at the same time are very low, therefore problem solved!

Being knowledgeable about your items not only means that you will always sell your client the things they need but you will usually be able to sell your client an alternative product. If you are out of cream conditioner then a leave in conditioner might work just as well, but only if you have the knowledge.

The Golden rule of retailing is simple — IT HAS TO BE IN STOCK

Nothing else matters if you have nothing to sell.

Years ago, when I was a retail manager this rule was at the core of almost everything I did. We sold around ten thousand different products in one department alone, and our maximum out of stock figure every morning at seven am was 10 product lines. Just ten items out of ten thousand. Even then the focus on that 10 lines was urgent, why are we out of stock? How do we stop being out of stock ever again? And how quickly can we get that product back on the shelf? I spend two hours, often more of every day just perfecting that availability. If we did not have it the customer could not buy it.

Most Salons have about thirty different items, more if they are holding two ranges and maybe have hair and beauty, but even a hundred different items are not difficult to keep in stock with a few simple systems.

> ## GOLDEN RULE
> "IF YOU DO NOT HAVE IT, YOU CANNOT SELL IT. NOTHING ELSE MATTERS IF YOU DO NOT HAVE THE PRODUCTS IN STOCK."

I CAN NOT AFFORD TO BUY THE PRODUCTS IN THE FIRST PLACE

I hear this from time to time and whilst for some failing salons it may feel like this, it is only used as a defense to the selling issue, because the salon owner cannot see how important selling products is. You say this to yourself when you think that selling is an optional part of your business, or an-add on. It is not an-add on it is what you do.

Customer service is how you make money.

If you went into a grocery store on the way home from work and the shelves were empty the owner would not say "I cannot afford to buy the stock", because that would mean that they were failing and about to close down their business. If you genuinely cannot afford stock, then you are always closer to failing and closing down. You may be closed before you get to the end of this book.

Some owners use this tactic to convince themselves that not selling products to clients is actually the right thing to do and if they can say to themselves that they have no spare money to buy stock then the matter must be out of their hands and carry on with the salon struggle.

We are back to the quicker I find an excuse the better I feel. Buying stock is not a spend. It is not like buying a TV for your house and putting it up on the wall. When you buy the TV, your money is now gone. Buying stock is an investment, you spend the money, you sell the product, now you have double the money. If you do not invest the money in products, you cannot sell them, and you cannot double your money.

> **INVEST IN STOCK**
> "STOCK IS NOT A COST TO THE BUSINESS, IT DOES NOT REDUCE THE AMOUNT OF MONEY YOU HAVE, IT ENABLES YOU TO DOUBLE THE AMOUNT OF MONEY THAT YOU HAVE."

I know what happens in underperforming salons, which unfortunately is most salons. When they focus and really try to sell products, they find that they are great at it after all. There feels like a lot more money in the business for a few weeks, so they use it to pay a long-standing bill or get that new sofa that they wanted. The core of the business remains the same and when it comes to replenishing the stock the money which has all been mixed up in the general account is no longer available.

This makes the salon owner feel as if it is too expensive to buy more products, product purchase feels like an inconvenience and a burden, when it is really a reward and a sign of success.

If you want to take customer service seriously you will always find the money for products.

Carl Hinder/Sell products or die (not) trying

IT IS THE CUSTOMERS FAULT THEY DO NOT BUY ANY PRODUCTS

Of course, the team do not say this to the clients face, at least that is a good start! But wait until they are in the staff room or the salon is empty! She did not have a clue what she wanted, I could have been there all day while she made up her mind, I think he was just wasting my time, he was not listening to a word I said.

This is something you never want to hear in your salon. No matter how true this may feel it says more about you than the client. This is where you need to move your mind set again, the client does not have a responsibility to buy something, the responsibility is all yours.

> **NOT SELLING?**
> "IT IS NEVER THE CUSTOMERS FAULT THAT THEY ARE NOT BUYING FROM YOU. NEVER."

This is a true quote, as I am sat here writing this book a Facebook forum has just beeped and this is the 100% real life quote.

"Why do clients not listen to aftercare advise!! Stresses me out!!"

These are actual replies

"Yup! Drives me potty ESPECIALLY when I have a printed aftercare sheet they have to read and sign☒🙊"

"Because they think they know better"

In a way it is great to see salon owners so disappointed that their clients are not taking their advice and also to see that they are disappointed that they did not make the sale. It tells me a lot about their passion. However, it also tells me that they have found a barrier, and excuse and they are prepared to prolificate it amongst anyone who will listen.

In this particular scenario where the client will not listen, or they think they know better, the obvious answer (to me) is that you have not asserted yourself as an expert in their eyes. That is your fault not the clients. There is a lot of focus on communicating the benefits of the product to the client, but it is how the product makes them feel that you need to focus on. These clients have never been sold to properly before, so you have to re-educate them too on this product/customer service journey.

You have to show responsibility and you have to take responsibility for everything that happens as an owner and everything that happens as a stylist. Until you take personal responsibility for the client, for their experience you cannot deliver awesome service, every time.

If you do not take responsibility for yourself, you cannot sell products and if you cannot sell products you cannot deliver the customer service levels that a successful salon and successful stylists need. You now know what your natural objections are, and you know what is coming from the client, you really do know what they are going to say as an objection or perhaps even what they are thinking. It is the ability to know what they are thinking that allows you to be prepared and being prepared for the objections means that you will have the answers ready.

It is never the client, it is always you.

If you had not bought this book, would it have been your fault or my fault for not convincing you that there is another, better way of delivering customer service, and that the benefits are so massive you would have been a fool to not change your business. My fault of course.

PART 4: HOW TO MAKE CHANGES

Carl Hinder/Sell products or die (not) trying

PRODUCTS

YOU NEED PRODUCTS

So far, we have looked into the background of product selling in the industry and how successful you would be if you sold products and improved your customer service by doing so. We have looked at all the reasons why you should sell products and we looked at all the barriers (excuses) that we have traditionally accepted and how they are damaging your business. We are not going to accept them anymore and this section is explains how you can change things.

Now that we know that we must sell and that there are no excuses we need to work out what you as a salon or a stylist needs to do to overcome the problems.

You Need Products!

This is easy. No products, no sales, no customer service.

You need two ranges of products, a branded product and your salon branded product. Let us start with the branded product. This will be different for every salon in terms of the target client and services you provide. If you already have an established salon and team this is a good starting point to get the team involved.

Carl Hinder/Sell products or die (not) trying

Do your research, narrow the ranges down to two that not only financially work for you, but offer good training support, marketing materials and hopefully some commitment to remaining salon exclusive, there are also other factors to be looking for. Do not take on a brand that is not salon exclusive and ditch any brands that go market wide.

A more recent development in salons has been the introduction of products that are part of MLMs, Multi-level marketing companies. An example of one of these companies would be 'Forever living'. Whilst, I am sure that many MLMs are fine organisations, their products are not salon exclusive, they are widely available and usually not developed for the professional market, such as your salon. They are not suitable for a salon environment where there are often complicated client issues involved. You are unlikely to have insurance cover in some instances too.

Even in the professional product sector some brands just go into large commercial outlets after being in the industry for a while, these are not usually the best brands to stick with and the general commercial nature can lower prices and quality of the product. Product diversion is well known in the industry, so too is "grey market' stock. This is where products are diverted away from their original intended market to other outlets and this can be a problem for salons trying to compete on image and price.

Carl Hinder/Sell products or die (not) trying

Although this can sometimes be temporary it usually floods the local market and devalues the salon brand rapidly. If this happens change product ranges.

Before you started to read this book, the old you would have said that you had built up a brand loyalty with your clients and now they will not want to change, the old you would have said that you could not financially afford to keep changing brands. The new you knows that changing brands is super exciting for the salon, for the stylists and the clients.

You will have another lease of life, with new training and new marketing. All you have to tell your clients is 'XBRAND' (the old brand) are now available at some supermarkets, we are concerned that the quality is going to drop, so we have worked really hard to find a product that is even better. We guarantee it will be what you need.' Financially, there is no risk for you if you are managing stock levels properly. First of all, a lot of companies will do some kind of exchange system, one for one or a credit note for new stock and take the rest away.

You can even sell some stock off at cost price, do some staff deals, develop them as gift packs or offer them to another salon. You see, there are no barriers.

Do not let the staff choose the range of products themselves, if you have ten staff you will have ten ranges to choose from. You will never choose a range that all the staff totally love, unless you only have one team member of course. Once you have chosen the two commercial brands that work for you as a business, then ask the supplier to send their representative to come and do a presentation to you and the team. Once the representative has gone make a decision, as a team and get the stock ordered.

> ## PRODUCT RANGES
> "HAVING TWO PRODUCT RANGES OFFERS YOUR CLIENT AN OPTION ON QUALITY AND AN OPTION ON PRICE."

The second piece of the product puzzle is the salon own brand range. Own brand is essential for profit and for marketing purposes. There will be two options open to you; firstly white label products. These are generic products that the supplier will put your salon name and brand on. For the Hairdressing and Barber sectors this is easy to do, cost effective and quick. Some of these small batch products are fantastic. All you need to do is find the company, a quick search on the forums or Google will throw up plenty, phone them and arrange for a set of samples.

Get two or three sets of samples, pay for more if you need to. Get using them in the salon for two weeks, then hold a team meeting to discuss the best company, both image (branding wise) and quality have to reflect your business. Again, do not expect the team to agree, but if they do the choice will be easy. Phone and make an order.

There is a second option when developing your own brand which is a lot more complicated and expensive, but if you have a high turnover salon or firm plans to grow, this is the option. Your own product range with your own formulae and licensing. You need to find a development lab and discuss what your needs are. Sometimes they already have formulae which can be altered but ensure that you plan plenty of time if you want a complete range.

This is definitely worth doing if your business is expanding quickly. The long-term profit margins are phenomenal if you have the right range and turnover.

In reality you are probably better off going white label if possible and developing the own formulae brand alongside, rather than waiting a year or two to finish the own brand project. Just ensure that the branding is similar so that the transition is smoother for the client.

Refer back to: Why you should sell products

This section gives key reasons why own brand products are essential in your business.

DISPLAYING THE PRODUCTS

Merchandising (displaying them). Is all about displaying items to make them more attractive as a purchase option to the client. How you merchandise will reflect the other values in your business, but also how the product looks, how it is grouped and even the price point is all part of your merchandised offer. If you have the space available a great retail area will communicate that you are professional and interested in real customer service. A separate area, that is easily accessible to all the clients will encourage browsing. Not everyone has plenty of space, but even a small well merchandised area will help the client and also ensure that the stylist knows where everything is, and what compliments each other so that they can select it quickly during a service. I could write another book on retail merchandising, but there is plenty of resource out there to help you become an expert on all the technical things you could do. These are the things that you must get right.

First of all, you need a merchandising stand; you can build one if you have the space, make it reflect your business and your values. Alternatively, you can usually get free standing ones from the product suppliers with your order, although they may cost extra.

You can also often purchase second hand ones through well-known auction sites. I would normally recommend one or two of these stands as they are usually high quality, are designed for the purpose and also, often have built in lighting.

Failing this, and depending on the design of your shop you can get something suitable from furniture stores, DIY outlets, office suppliers etc. The key thing is that it is safe, stable, and can accommodate all the items.

Aesthetically, you should have all the large items on the bottom and the small items on the top, good for stability too, but this does not usually make shopping sense. So, you want to get all your products into logical groups. As an example: the hair care color range should be grouped together. Then put them in order starting from the left, put the colors shampoos together, then the color conditioners together, then the color treatments. If they are not all the same size, then ideally the products on the left would slope down to the smaller products on the right.

Repeat this with each category. The quantity of stock on display is also important; shelves need to be faced up, brought to the edge of the shelf.

Carl Hinder/Sell products or die (not) trying

The actual quantities that you need will depend on the size of your turnover, but 3 of each item, often called SKU's (Stock Keeping Unit) of the slow selling products and 6 of each of the faster ones should be good to get you started.

You will hear a lot of talk about how to use eye level merchandising, and how it is the hot spot. It is, but it is not the most important thing, the most important thing is that you have everything in stock, all of the time. However, the eye level shelf or shelves should be between 4' and 6' high. This is where most people browse from in the high street or a department store. This is where you would put high value, high profit lines if you have them. However, your products need to be grouped first and foremost by category, the profit margin will be similar throughout, so just use this space for popular or promotional items and change them regularly. Do not forget that 99% of your product sales are going to be done on stylist recommendation so complying with every merchandising rule is not as essential as being neatly presented, and having full, clean shelves with products that are priced. When it comes to displaying gifts like expensive shaving sets, hair straighteners etc. you need a display area, do not leave then in the stock room because you think they will get stolen.

Get them on display, (even if it is just the packaging) with a big sign saying what they are and the price. If they are branded gifts get the posters in the windows so that passing traffic can see that you are the go-to place for this item. When you go to a market stall in most countries the marketeer shouts out about their product, the ones they need to sell, they shout the price and people respond, you need to do the same, you need to let you customer know what you have for them! If they do not know about it, they will not be able to buy it.

Extracting products from the ranges on a weekly or monthly basis can be a good idea so that the team are focused on talking about something new. Having hot spots or touch points around the salon can really help promote this. These hot spots are area that all clients visit or look at, such as the reception desk, coffee table or in between the workstations.

Key promotions like the 'product of the week' needs to be an item that offers itself to the majority of your clients so that you have a wide audience to discuss it with. There is little point in promoting a colour shampoo if only ten percent of your clients have colours with you. Our online course goes into more detail on how and why to merchandise correctly.

PRICING THE PRODUCTS

Sometimes known as marking up, is normally a legal requirement, it certainly is in the UK, so lets us get it done anyway. You essentially have a number of options, you can price the item, or you can put up a label/shelf talker, you can also use a menu or list, but it has to be clear and it has to be very near the products it represents. I would always manually put a price label on the bottom of the item, this encourages the client to pick the product up from the shelf or even at the work station, and once it is in their hand you know you have a buying signal! It also saves the stylist from saying the price which sometimes feels like a bit of a trauma! As price is unimportant, the stylist can concentrate on the benefits to the client. I would also add in shelf talkers (promotional signs) or a menu and a POS (Point of sale) sign for promotional products.

The actual price itself will be salon specific, but it should be at least double the cost price, and do not forget that a RRP is just a recommended price, which you are free to ignore. As a general rule of thumb you will want your own brand at a higher level than the standard brand.

Not only does this reflect on your business as being a premium business but it also gives you plenty of margin to do price promotions if needed, and you can trade down to the standard item if necessary. Whilst price cutting anywhere in your business should be strictly limited, there can be times when selling multiple purchases, such as buy 2 get the 3rd free can be a real boost to the business without effecting longer term sales. This is great for the Christmas/Holiday period. Summer holidays or January sales when everyone is switched on to the price reduction marketing in almost every other business. Do not try and maintain low product prices to encourage long term sales, this does not work.

Still do not believe that price has no effect on long term sales? Take my Product Price Challenge and put my advice to the test.

PRODUCT PRICE CHALLENGE

"CHOOSE ANY SALON PRODUCT, WRITE DOWN HOW MANY YOU SOLD LAST WEEK. REDUCE THE PRICE BY 25%. LEAVE IT AT THAT PRICE FOR TWELVE WEEKS THEN CHECK YOUR SALES OF THAT PRODUCT ON THE TWELFTH WEEK. I GUARANTEE IT WILL BE THE SAME, IF NOTHING ELSE IN YOUR BUSINESS HAS CHANGED."

FUNDING THE PRODUCTS

Some salon owners do not purchase stock and they do not keep stock levels up. I do not think anyone would argue that if you have not got an item in stock you cannot sell it, and long gone are the days when you can get it in for them. It needs to be there, right here, right now. As a salon owner, you say or think that you cannot afford them, but the reality is you cannot afford to ignore product sales and customer service. I am always perplexed by salon owners who have no stock but when challenged they tell me that they have sold out. That immediately tells me that you were successful at selling, made extra sales and profit but did not want to repeat the success. That is not natural business behavior (outside of our industry), it is not natural behavior for a human being. Normally, when we do something that is good for us, we see the rewards we want to repeat it.

If you are having cash flow issues, then it is because the overall business is in poor health not because you are selling too many products and you cannot afford to keep replacing them. If you have exhausted all other options to increase your cash flow and there is definitely no money in the business, this is what you do:

Put everything into place that I have described in this book, take the course too if you still are not sure.

Firstly, buy (order) the stock. Most companies will give you between 30 and 90 days to pay. Then pay the invoice for the stock on a credit card, this will give you another 30 plus days, most cards give you 55 days before you get charged any interest, if you time it right, but do check on your card to be sure. We know that you have everything in place in this book before you ordered them, so before they arrive you are obsessed with product selling.

Once the stock arrives you and the team must work vigorously to sell these products. As you do, take the money from the till or the bank account each day and put it separate from the general service sales.

If you need the money to pay a general bill out of this fund then remember it is not the product sales that are failing, it is the rest of the business. So, do not do it. Keeping this money in a separate account until your retail offer is established, will show you how well product selling is performing and growing for you. If you are pushing the product sale customer service culture you will need to order more stock quite soon. With this fund system it will not feel as if the product purchases are a burden on your finances.

Carl Hinder/Sell products or die (not) trying

It is extremely important that with this system that you pay these bills on time otherwise you will stop the product flow, because the supplier will withhold your order. Keep reinvesting this money in new retail products, things that you can sell, not things that you can use. Get a second range as soon as you can, and then invest in the third layer of stock, electrical goods like straighteners, hairdryers, gift packs etc. This third layer will need special attention. Once you have a solid operation of course you can use one account, but this is the system to resolve a common complaint.

Carl Hinder/Sell products or die (not) trying

THE THIRD RANGE OF PRODUCTS

This is your stealth range. This is where the rules completely change, indeed I would almost say that there are no rules for these products. These items are mainly gifts and whilst you can sell them all year around, they are essential for the golden quarter, Christmas or the holiday season. You need to focus on gifts. Your client is more likely to be buying these for someone else than themselves. As an example; if you are a Barber Shop you need to have gifts for the clients partner and friends, so maybe more female orientated products.

Of course, you as a Barber shop need male orientated products too. This is a good opportunity to sell higher value items like hair straighteners, hairdryers, wands etc. as well as product gift packs, perfume and of course *gift vouchers. Electrical goods need to be premium brands, and they can sometimes need a slightly different approach to low value items. In my personal experience men can also need extra value added to the product. So, if you have hair straighteners at £/S150 then you may wish to offer clients the chance to take advantage of your installment scheme, let them pay each time they come in, collecting them maybe Christmas week, or for Valentines day.

Have one product ready wrapped, bow, even a tag for them to write out their message, something as small as that could easily clinch the deal! This is adding more value.

FOCUS ON GIFTS

"BE CREATIVE AND FIND GIFT IDEAS THAT WILL HELP YOUR CLIENTS SOLVE THEIR PROBLEMS, EVERYDAY COULD BE A GIFT DAY."

Having premium brands in your salon that are well advertised is not only essential but expected. Whilst I was in the process of writing this book, I came across a very interesting situation on a builders (construction) forum, which consists of nearly all men. One of them asked where he could get GHD hair straighteners for his wife for Christmas. There were 346 replies, over 300 men said, 'Any reputable salon near you should sell them.' Without being disparaging to my fellow men, but if the marketing machine has penetrated that deep into the male sector, then the female sector will also be hugely aware of where they should be buying these goods. As with all product sales you are solving a problem for the client, often the problem is that they just do not know what to get or they have left it very late and the special occasion is upon them.

The difference here is that you need much less emphasis on need. They may need to solve the problem, in so much as they have to get one from somewhere soon, but you do not need to tailor it to the need of the person they are buying it for. Of course, you can try and match your gift solutions with the future recipient, but it is not essential. If in doubt when selling a gift item, just SELL IT.

Very few people complain about a gift they receive and even fewer identify that the retailer (you) is responsible for the gift choice. So just sell it, rule free selling. Do not skip this part of selling, Christmas as a whole month is no longer highly lucrative for just service sales, indeed I know many salons that are busier in May and July, but that depends on you service mix. The product gift selling part can be a massive boost to sales in the Christmas window.

*I mention gift vouchers as a product sale even though they are usually redeemed on services because they are normally purchased for special occasions and they do not need to be tailored to the individual, although checking what their intended purpose might be, can be an opportunity to trade up, (maybe they are intended to be used for a course of fillers, or electrolysis etc. then a £5 voucher just will not do it). I would always have the gift voucher not redeemable against products and no change given as part of its conditions.

When a client comes in for their service, it is going to feel free or low cost to them, and to you too unfortunately, even though you have had the money. That feeling that they do not need to pay today, at least not full price now puts them in the psychological position of being able to spend today, and that means selling them products that they need. These product sales will also support your cashflow for what feels like a free service.

Tip — If you are having gift vouchers physically made only do them in high denominations, starting at £/S 20, then £/S 50 then a £/S 100, people will always trade up. The client may ask for £/S5 or £/S 10 but tell them they start at £/S 20. If your average service is over £/S 100 then start at £/S 50.

Always put a redeem by date on the vouchers, but in all honestly, within reason I would not enforce it. You have had the money so you have not lost anything, but the date will deter some people from redeeming the voucher at some unexpected busy period in the future. In some countries there is an automatic 5-year redemption period so check your country or State. In the UK, according to gov.uk 6% of all gift vouchers are never redeemed, which is a great profit bonus for businesses.

ORDERING THE PRODUCTS

It does not matter how awesome your team are, or how stunning your salon looks, if you do not have products in stock, then you cannot sell them. Do not rely on the system of telling your client that you are sorry that it is out of stock, that you will order it today and it should be in sometime next week, and of course you will call them when it arrives. That is pretty much a lost sale. You have to remember two things.

1. We live in an age of instant gratification,
'I want it now.'

2. You are there to solve their problems, so going home without their color shampoo is not solving their problem, it is giving them a problem.

So, you need an ordering system. Your orders need to be done weekly, preferably at 8am (or as soon as you open) on the first day that you open each week, usually a Monday or Tuesday. Now block out 60 minutes at from 9am in your diary if you are doing the order or go to the appointment system and book out the first hour from the person who is doing the order, book that out for the next two years or even forever.

The nominated person or product champion now has an hour to create the order and phone or e mail it to the correct supplier.

Most salons have software that can generate them an order. These are usually completely wrong, because it requires a lot of human input and there are a lot a variables. The software-based system relies on someone inputting or confirming the order, all items being scanned out correctly, all salon use or giveaways being stock adjusted, and regular stock checks in case there is theft or human error. If you have someone who is tech smart then by all means use the software, but my system is better and this system is fool proof.

On an A4 pad:

1) Write down your product on the left-hand side (Col 1)

2) Write down your commitment level alongside the product (Col 2)

The commitment level is how many of each item you need in stock?

You calculate this by working out how many you sell and then double that figure so that you have two weeks stock on hand. You need two weeks stock so that you do not sell out when you have unexpected sales, the ordering person goes sick or the supplier is temporarily out of stock.

Carl Hinder/Sell products or die (not) trying

Just start with display SKU's (the amount that the shelf holds) if you are just starting out and you can adjust them over the next few weeks. However, if you are trying to be more accurate not all the products ordered have to fit on the shelf. If you sell twelve a week but there is only space for six you will need another storage area.

Product (col 1)   Commitment (Col 2)

E.g.   Dandruff shampoo   12

The next thing you need is to add another two columns, the first for Stock on hand (SOH) (Col 3)

This is the stock you actually have on the morning of ordering, on the shelves and any in storage.

The last column is the actual order (Col 4)

This is the amount you will be ordering with the supplier.

Product	Commitment	SOH	Order
E.g. Dandruff shampoo	12	10	2

Once you have the SOH figure you just take it away from the commitment level. This gives you the number of items that you need to order.

If you keep selling out of an item, you increase the commitment level by a couple and if you are hardly ever selling an item you lower the commitment level by a couple until the stock level comes down. It is important that only one person is allowed to change the commitment levels, usually the salon owner. Having all staff involved will cause chaos.

Once all the areas have been done you just phone or e mail your order through to the supplier (or use the order app) and when the stock arrives you check it off against the delivery note and fill up the shelves. Repeat process.

Important: Do not let a sales representative order anything on your behalf or let them tell you that you must order monthly. You do not, and if they insist find another supplier.

If you are a large salon operation you may choose to operate monthly to gain better discounts, but for most salons getting to grips with products sales, weekly is the best option

You can see a mockup of the order page towards the back of the book, which you can copy or modify for your own salon purposes.

Carl Hinder/Sell products or die (not) trying

We also have the order page set up as an Excel spread sheet available **free of charge** which you can download at www.salon-help.co.uk or e mail info@salon-help.co.uk

ORDER WEEKLY
"FOR MAXIMUM CONTROL AND CASH FLOW ORDER WEEKLY, ON THE SAME DAY EACH WEEK."

Carl Hinder/Sell products or die (not) trying

STAFF

STAFF TRAINING

So, you have stock, well presented, priced and merchandised properly. You also have all your stealth products and vouchers, you are now armed, but not ready to sell. Before we even look at the challenges that are happening every day with regards to product selling, let us make a stand and make sure that you have everything in place within your salon team.

Without staff training you have a very unstable ship, literally imagine a ship where no one was trained. The ship would at best go around in circles until it ran out of fuel, or just simply end up beached or sank through a lack of control. Even if the ship kept going because the captain knew what they were doing but the deck hands did not know how to fuel the ship, maintain the ship or dock it in port, it is only ever going to end one way, in failure.

You need to look at education in the way you look at fuel in a vehicle, you have to keep putting it in to keep it moving. Put in more fuel than you think you will ever need.

In your salon, or even if you work by yourself you have to keep developing yourself, every day you must move forward, even the slightest bit will make you better than before. In salons we are not too bad at skills training, stylists will often put themselves on training courses, watch videos or ask for advice. However, we need to put as much emphasis, if not more, into every other facet. From how to answer the telephone, do a consultation and especially how to deliver real customer service, including product sales.

In larger teams you need to identify the most positive member of the team and train them first. Train them how to sell, train them to have outstanding product knowledge, do the ordering, fill the stands and eventually train other staff. This could be a receptionist, a manager or even a junior, but they have to be the most positive person that you have.

PRODUCT KNOWLEDGE

"PRODUCT KNOWLEDGE WILL HELP YOU ASSURE THE CLIENT THAT THEY ARE MAKING THE RIGHT DECISION. ASSURANCE IS THE GREATER PART OF SELLING."

Carl Hinder/Sell products or die (not) trying

Product knowledge: in itself will not get the team to sell products, but you cannot convince or assure a client if you do not have amazing product knowledge. Every member of a team has to buy into what they are selling. We know that it is impossible to have a team that loves every product, it just does not happen, it is human nature to have different preferences. What you or the team need to do is first of all is buy into why product selling is essential to the client and the business, then buy into what they are selling.

To enable everyone to buy into a range of products without having to have a range for each stylist, each member of the team needs to find three things that they like about the product. They might like or hate ten things about it, but they must find three that they like, and to begin they can be anything at all. They might like the smell, the consistency, the size of the bottle, the flip top lid, the way it works, how long it lasts, that its eco- friendly, not tested on animals, absolutely anything at all. Each member of the team needs to go through every product and write down exactly what they like about each product and then learn those things that they like. You can even do that in the salon if you are working by yourself. When they or you have a gap in between clients they should get their list out and learn the three things like they are the most important values in the world. Discuss them at team meetings, go to the local bar and have a quiz.

Whatever you do immerse yourself in product knowledge.

Product knowledge can be re-enforced by getting support from the suppliers and you need to secure this once or twice a year. It is an important commitment from any new suppliers that you take on. Sometimes your team just needs to hear a different voice. There are now lots of online resource available too, there is no need to stop learning. You cannot afford to stop learning, you have to keep developing yourself, your skills and your knowledge.

Your in-salon, training needs to change too. Many salons have weekly or monthly training sessions sometimes during work hours sometimes outside of normal trading and we focus almost solely on practical skills. A key mistake is that we treat the models who have come in for a massage, facial, haircut or any other service as models, or worse as friends and family. No matter what connection they have to the salon you need to treat them in every way like a regular client. Practice everything, practice greeting them, doing the consultation, escorting them to the area, put on the right music, light the candles, listen to their problems, and find their needs. Recommend what services they need in the future and practice your product selling technique until it is an instinct. You must practice product selling scenarios, on your own and with the team, if indeed you have one.

RECRUITMENT

The recruitment process and interview.

It is great to start training on your existing team, if you have one, but give a thought to new staff as well.

The next time you do an interview discuss selling products as a part of customer service. I would ask them, Would you sell a client a product if it made them happy? Are there any times that you would refuse to sell a product to a client if they needed it? And how would you know if they needed it?" These questions may feel challenging for some interviewers and candidates. If there is not a willingness to adopt this style of customer service from the candidate, then do not employ them. You may frighten off a few candidates too, that are not willing to overcome the challenge that comes with great customer service. Great news, you have saved yourself a lot of time trying to change them when they join. Of course, you can expect candidates to feel unsure about a change in the way they work, because they have been brain washed by the anti-selling, anti-pushy brigade over a number of years, so do not discount everyone who looks a bit unsure, but at least if there is a willingness at the interview, then you can help them with training and coaching and you can both be successful.

Carl Hinder/Sell products or die (not) trying

THE CONTRACT & INDUCTION

You have found the best candidates to join your team, and they are ready to start. The first part of the induction is to sit down and go through their contract and terms and conditions, line by line. Do not give them the contract and handbook to take home and read (unless they are under 18 years of age, and their guardian may need to sign it), they will never bring it back, and probably never read it either.

Go through every line in the contract and terms and conditions, explaining it so that they fully understand. Make sure that you have something about product selling in your handbook or type something up and add it in. Just a line or two that explains that product selling is compulsory and part of the expected customer service levels for your salon, even get them to circle it and initial it, you do not want any doubt about your selling standards. It is always advisable to get your contracts from industry bodies, that way you will always be legally covered for any major issues. Writing your own is a false economy. If you have "rent a chair" workers or "booth renters," unfortunately you cannot get them involved in the product selling culture as they do not work for you. You may be able to sell them your own brand products at a preferential rate.

Next, dedicate a day to training the new team member on the product selling process in your salon. I know the pressures that salons feel under when they have a new team member, they just want to get them onto the sales floor doing the service.

This is plain bad management. Set aside a week or more for the induction, at least one day dedicated to product selling. If you have a large team the salon owner does not have to be the trainer, but it has to be the person who has a passion for selling, otherwise the selling energy will not be passed onto the new starter. If you can develop an individual as your product champion you will find it easier to get the team to follow them, as well as this being a great role for their self-development. The product champion can also be responsible for ordering stock.

> ## DO A PROPER INDUCTION
> "STARTING A NEW MEMBER OF STAFF ON THE SALES FLOOR ON THEIR FIRST DAY (WEEK,) IS PLAIN BAD MANAGEMENT."

TARGETS

There is a business saying that states what gets measured gets done and this is almost always true. It just means if you hold yourself or someone accountable for a target or a goal, they will work towards it and it will usually get achieved. If you say to your children, "I want to see your homework before you go to bed," they will almost certainly dash off and do it. If you are going to get married you set a date, that way you both turn up and it gets done! The same with selling.

So, all the team need individual targets.

First of all, 100% of clients can be sold to. You just need to find out what their problem is and then solve it. You must not allow yourself or your team to ever think that there is someone who cannot be sold to. You just need to work harder at finding out what they need. However, you cannot sell to 100% of clients every week. But, as a guide every single client should have bought something at least once in a three-month period, if they have not bought anything at all it is time to investigate why. The answer is with the stylist not the customer.

LOOK AT YOUR OWN PERFORMANCE

"IT IS DOWN TO YOU TO SELL TO THE CLIENT. IT IS NOT THE CLIENTS RESPONSIBILITY TO BUY FROM YOU."

When setting a target for overall products sold, do not set a financial one, (unless it is for a short-term incentive) otherwise the stylists will focus on electrical goods and gifts only, which will defeat the object of delivering the best possible customer service.

The target that must be set is a percentage of customers in their column or a percentage of customers that visit your salon. The target that you are aiming for is 30% (3 out of every10) of all clients purchase a product every day. After six months of developing retail in your business you move it to 40%. (4 out of every 10). That is just the target.

Now you need to measure the performance and hold each of the stylists accountable, but they can also hold themselves accountable. Each member of the team should have a sheet or a screen that they personally fill out every day before they go home. This record sets out how many clients they delivered service to, how many they should have sold products to how many products they sold.

Carl Hinder/Sell products or die (not) trying

That is pretty easy information to record, but if you prefer you can use or copy our version which is printed towards the back of the book, or you can get the excel spreadsheet version for free from our website: www.salon-help.co.uk or request a copy by e mail from info@salon-help.co.uk

By completing this sheet daily before they go home, they will know how well they are doing, so that they understand their performance without you having to chase them all day, every day, and of course it means that they can work on their strategy for the following day if required. It is also essential for them to know their performance before you meet with them.

Now it is your turn, if you are a salon manager or owner. This is the most important thing that a salon owner can do. Without doing this part you will not be successful at selling products, it will not work! You must do this. Book out 15 minutes with every member of staff, every week to have one to one meetings. Put them into the appointment system for the next 12 months, now write those same appointments into your diary, Do Not change them.

When you leave on a Saturday afternoon you need the figures in your hand of what each person has done, including yourself if you are a stylist owner.

Write them down on the sales sheet or print them off. **Your commitment is to meet with each member of staff every single week of your life.**

Do not sit down, do not get coffee. Stand up, seriously, the meeting will be shorter, and all parties will pay attention. At the meeting ask the stylist how they performed on **customer service** last week, not how did product selling go, "how did you perform on customer service last week"?

The answer you are looking for is, "I did X number of customers and I sold X number of products" If they can give you their success rate in percentage then great, but often in our industry a percentage does not always mean much to some team members. They do know that for every 10 clients that they have they should have sold a minimum of three products, and they really do need to understand that.

If you want to work a percentage out, you can just take the number of products, divide that by the number of customers and multiply by 100 for your answer

10 products

÷ 52 clients

= 0.2 x 100

= 20%

Or you can download our excel spreadsheet version for free from our website www.salon-help.co.uk or request a copy by e mail from info@salon-help.co.uk which will work it out for you.

If they do not know what a percentage is then have the figures ready for them and show them how to work, it out for next week.

"You did 20% last week, you had two hundred clients and you sold to 40 of them!"

> ## PROGRESS TOGETHER
> "WHAT CAN I DO TO HELP YOU? WHAT ARE YOU GOING TO DO TO HELP YOURSELF?"

Now you need to praise them if they are improving and ask them what you can do to help them improve their customer service. Usually it will be some form of advice or training.

"What can I do to help you improve your customer service levels?"

If they fail to deliver good or improving customer service after 6 weeks and you have completed all the training to a high standard then at the next meeting ask them "What are YOU going to do to improve your customer service?" Ask them for actions that they are going to take before the next meeting. Document their commitments.

"What are you going to do to improve your customer service levels?"

If there is regular improvement every week then keep driving the levels with this individual.

Do this for another 6 weeks.

The reason we approach this with a zero-tolerance attitude is twofold.

1) 12 weeks is the normal probationary period for a new starter, and you do not want to be engaging in a permanent contract if they are not showing significant signs of good customer service levels. Remember, because it is a percentage of visits it is proportional to their experience and client base. If they only have three clients in a week and sell to one, they are achieving over 30% success rate! It is tough, but it is fair.

2) Whether they are new or existing staff you must remember that this is about customer service. Product sales and customer service are the same thing.
You would not accept any member of the team delivering poor customer service in any other part of the business; you would not accept colour dye getting on clients clothes, someone rushing a massage to go on their lunch, nails peeling off in record time, or someone being cut to bits during a shave etc, and let it just carry on for three or four months, no way, you would have it sorted as soon as possible. So, the question is: Why would you let staff, or yourself give awful customer service by not helping clients with their individual needs and supplying them with the products they need. Why should this go on any longer than any other poor service. It should not.

If you and the team understand the concept of customer service your team should continue to develop, but ultimately be prepared to utilise the disciplinary system to drive home the message.

There is a mis-understanding in the industry, that considers a disciplinary hearing to be the same as disciplinary action.

The purpose of a hearing is NOT to take action against an individual so that you move them one step closer to leaving your employment. The purpose of the hearing is to formally discuss the issues, listen and hear what the employee has to say, and after consideration agree actions that will improve the performance of the employee in a reasonable time period. Some of those actions will be things that the salon owner will do to support the employee in improving their performance. Do not be afraid to use them if all other methods have failed.

In my experience this is a highly unlikely position to be in and should be avoided if the stylist attitude is improving, and they are a positive influence, even in the smallest way. This is a fairly robust way of driving the change, and in an industry where you rarely hold anyone accountable for fear of them leaving and not finding a replacement, I know this approach will be received with a big frown, because like selling it requires you to challenge yourself. It can sound harsh or unfair, but unless you are intense about changing the salon culture then it will not change, and the non-selling culture will drag on forever. Get focused.

Carl Hinder/Sell products or die (not) trying

If you are reading this and thinking "I have awesome customer service through product sales, and I never disciplined anyone", Congratulations, that is the way it should be, but also remember you are in the one percent of salons, perhaps in the world, that take selling seriously. This book is for the other ninety-nine percent.

Carl Hinder/Sell products or die (not) trying

Carl Hinder/Sell products or die (not) trying

COMMISSION & INCENTIVES

As with all ambitions in life there is a reward or a penalty whether you want it or not. There is nothing in life that does not have this rule. Eat properly you are rewarded with improved health, eat junk food you are going to be penalised with cholesterol or weight gain. Study at school you get a better outlook on life, you are able to take opportunities that come your way, do not study and you will have less friends, less opportunities in life and probably less money for you and your family. The same with selling products; deliver great service and you get rewarded, deliver poor service and you are going to have less financial reward.

Let us give these stylists a reward.

Commission: I would not do commission on product sales.

Commission on products rarely works, and if your reason for selling the product is the commission on it then you are selling it for the wrong reasons. Salons usually use a low commission on products, maybe 5% or 10% when is often not very motivational for the stylist as that can be as under a £/$ 1, which does not connect with a cash hungry stylist, even though cumulatively the end of month figure might be quite good.

As an owner you are just losing margin and profit on products that need to be sold anyway.

It is important to keep returning to the core of product selling, and that is, you should only be selling a product because a client NEEDS it, after all you are trying to solve a problem and driving awesome customer service at the same time.

Clients are also certainly put off buying anything that is commission driven, and this can create distrust between the client and the stylist. Do not put commission on products.

REWARD WINNERS

"AS WITH ALL AMBITIONS IN LIFE THERE IS A REWARD OR A PENALTY WHETHER YOU WANT IT OR NOT."

Incentives can often work, because they are more flexible than straight commission. They usually work although they may serve the purpose of encouraging stylists to sell items that are not required, just like commission, but incentives can be better controlled and can make the working environment interesting and engaging, so the risk is certainly worth it. The key to incentives or rewards is to have short time periods to measure, certainly no more than 1 month.

Carl Hinder/Sell products or die (not) trying

Competition based rewards can be great for morale but try targeting these at gift type products such as hair straighteners or gift vouchers so that if the clients are over sold, they are still going home with something that is useful, solves a problem, and if they do not need it for personal use, customer service is not affected.

An example of a short incentive, probably one month:

If you sell a well branded electrical item like GHD's, then you could just offer one of them as a prize for the person who sells the most of that item in that month, or one for everyone who sells more than twelve in December. The more winners you have the better, but at the same time do not reward people for failure, otherwise you are teaching them to fail and not succeed.

> **WINNERS**
> "THE MORE WINNERS YOU CAN CREATE THE BETTER, ENCOURAGE DEVELOPMENT, BIT DO NOT REWARD FAILURE."

I recently helped my ten-year-old son to do his homework project, which was a stand-up power point presentation. He wanted to understand why older people generally criticised younger people over their work ethic, and maybe he had heard me complaining too? We decided that he was probably referring to 'millennials,' so we broke things down. In the end we decided that it was not the millennials fault for the way they behaved and in summary agreed that most millennials wanted a different working environment and reward to previous generations and that the work place had failed to identify that and change.

Yes, he is 10 years old.

But the thing that really registered with him, with hardly any prompting at all was that (the past twenty years or so, he does not know that) he realised that children at school were rewarded for failing. Come last in a race and get a 'participation medal,' and if you win, you also get a medal. Not only misleading these children that losing will be rewarded, but undervaluing achievement.

At the same time. My 12 year old daughter became a bronze medalist in the Welsh Karate Championships, she was happy with a bronze, it was a great achievement, but could not understand why the two girls ahead of her had higher rewards when earlier she had beaten them both to the punch.

Carl Hinder/Sell products or die (not) trying

Admittedly a little too hard perhaps, as both girls cried and my daughter was scored against. In Karate terms it was all fair and it is all about control, so no qualms there, but the Silver and Gold medalist had learnt to win by being weaker (if there was no crying there would have been no penalty for their opposition).

Of course, in the workplace some of these millennials (maybe it is you?) find it difficult to function, because they now, no longer get rewarded for failure or participating, they only get rewarded for success. Millennials or not, you cannot afford to affirm failure as acceptable, at best you will end up as average, and who wants to be average? Fortunately, in a salon you do not automatically have to have losers. With good management, the whole team can be successful, and that needs encouragement and reward.

This team approach, and incentive is especially good for peak trading periods when most of the team are working together. However, team incentives can be operated annually or bi annually with some success, but it requires a lot of energy to keep the team focused, which is why monthly or shorter incentives work so well. If you decide to do an annual incentive, you still need the weekly and monthly incentives to keep everyone engaged. An annual incentive/reward would normally have to be fairly substantial, and that means a financial outlay for you.

For this reason, I would combine service sales and product sales together so that the whole business is moving forward not just your customer service standards.

However, there is one essential rule for the longer, larger incentives, and that is the team must choose what they want for themselves, otherwise, I guarantee it will not work. Give them a rough monetary value and ask them to choose what they would like to do. If they all hate the cold there is no point having a skiing weekend in the mountains. If they do not like alcohol there is no point having a weekend in a top vineyard. **They must choose it.**

Cash incentives can be great, although you or the stylist may have some tax implications which can take the shine off the prize, so if the winner wants to spend the money on a particular gift it may be better for you and the winning staff member to buy that for them, depending on your local tax laws. Either way it is a great way to reward more people.

INCENTIVES

"TEAM INCENTIVES MUST BE CHOSEN BY THE TEAM, OR THE TEAM WILL REJECT THE INCENTIVE."

You do not want the same winner every week!

Carl Hinder/Sell products or die (not) trying

If you want to focus the team on their Customer service target one month then a cash prize might be suitable, especially if it is around an event like Mothers Day or Fathers Day. Rewarding team members for achieving their 30% customer service level for a short time may work to keep the interest in the salon and a focus on what they are trying to achieve, but I would use this with caution, otherwise, as before, the reason for selling will move away from its purpose of driving customer service.

You can also do a daily cash incentive say one day a month when the whole team are in on a busy day, one of things we used to do was wrap a £/$ 20 note/bill in a piece of silver foil, every time someone made a sale they passed the silver foil to that person, at the end of the day the person holding the foil gets to keep the money. The client must not know what everyone is passing around, or indeed what they are laughing hysterically about, especially in that last hour.

Whatever the incentive/rewards that you use, make sure they are very frequent and well publicised. Use charts, graphs and maybe have a closed Facebook page, all out of view of the clients and above all celebrate the winners.

These systems also work for service sales, but do not combine the two too often, as staff will start drifting away from customer service sales, selling products.

> ## CLOSING THE SALE
> "THE CLIENT BUYS A PRODUCT ONCE THE VALUE OF THE ITEM EXCEEDS THE PRICE."

THE STRUCTURE

If you are a salon owner you must realise that the quality of your team is a direct result of how you personally behave, what you demand of them, but more importantly what you demand of yourself. That does not mean that you need to deliver a service at a high standard so that they can copy you, many salon owners are not stylists themselves, which is often a business strength. It means that if you are not prepared to create the right environment they cannot operate in the right environment. You must take responsibility for them.

By now you should have everything in place to sell, and like all other parts of your business you need a structure. You already have a structure for:

Ordering

Merchandising

Product knowledge

Target setting & accountability

Now you need a sales structure.

Carl Hinder/Sell products or die (not) trying

THE COMMUNICATION STRUCTURE

This is about what you verbally say, it is your script, like when an actor walks onto a film set. They have learnt the moves and the words. The best actors have learnt the words, but they do not sound like robots, they learn to adlib and often get the script changed.

Write down a few sentences that you can learn and use with every client, like when you go on a foreign holiday and want to communicate with the locals. You only need a verbal structure to get you started, as you become more experienced you will work out what the clients respond to best.

Some selling can be done before the client is even due to have their service done. I mentioned earlier about telling people over the phone about the exciting new products that you cannot wait to show them, as well as social media and your website. These are all pre-selling.

Another great opportunity is at the pre-consultation. These are the consultations that we do before the service day, usually things like hair colour, hair extensions, skin treatments, micro-pigmentation etc. These consultations need to be documented, indeed they need to have a well-developed proforma that is usually on paper, but of course can be digital.

The key to a great consultation is to ask plenty of open-ended questions and gather information which you write down.

The more information that you can gather the nearer the service will be to the clients needs and expectations. As an example, asking a client about their holiday plans, may result in the decision to move away from the intense red colour that the client first indicated. The Sun, sea and chlorine in the swimming pool are all going to seriously damage the hair and colour, maybe you need to advise other options or maybe a solution to the problem. A large section of your consultation needs to be dedicated to product advice, this will sow the seed for the day of the visit and make your service day so much smoother.

In this section we would probably be advising on a colour shampoo, possibly with pigment, a leave in conditioner with UV filters and depending on the length of the trip an intense treatment. Adding some free advice like wear a swimming cap, stay in the shade etc. can all help. These need to be written down along with the agreed colours, patch test requirements, and the dozens of other pieces of important information.

Carl Hinder/Sell products or die (not) trying

At this stage all you need to say is "the colour that you have chosen is really intense, it is going to look absolutely amazing on you, so to keep it looking good with all that sun and water you are going to need these products to help you look after it".

Get the products out, educate the client on why they will benefit her and how they work, get her to hold them, read them, smell them. Then tell the client "you do not need them today, but I can run through them again when you come in for the colour", now take them away from her, as if she is not allowed them. People always want things more when they cannot have them.

You can do this with all sit-down consultations.

This process can be applied to most services. If a client is having a course of Botox, then the client needs to be aware of potential bruising if they are going to an event, to refrain from vigorous exercise, not to have a hot shower, stay away from alcohol etc. the time the treatment will last and of course the skin care kit that they can use after twenty four hours to make the effects last longer.

You can apply it to a quality shave in the barbershop. One of the key things when doing a shaving consultation is to understand how that person currently shaves, what is their shaving routine.

Then using your expertise, you will be able to tell them how to get better shaving results, like shaving in a hot shower, the direction of the blade travel and using cold water to close the pores. But essentially, they may need professional equipment (maybe a brush) and professional products, shaving cream, facial wash, toner and moisturizer.

If you do not educate these clients who will?

Examples of open-ended questions to use at a consultation:

"Tell me about any holiday or event plans that you have"

"Tell me more about your career lifestyle"

"How does this problem make you feel"

"Describe how you would like it to look"

"What are the main benefits of this treatment to you"

"Talk me through the reasons why you have decided to have this done"

"What did you like about the way it was done last time"

Essentially questions that do not require a yes or no answer. Let the client talk.

Carl Hinder/Sell products or die (not) trying

If you are a serious salon, and when I say that, I mean serious about making money over a sustained period but not dying from old age whilst waiting for your financial rewards, then you need to go to the next step with conviction.

Once the consultation has finished you need to add up all the services and products and quote the client the overall price "your overall service with us, for everything we have discussed is £/$ xxxx, now when would be the best time to get you booked in? You must resist the temptation to say and give separate prices for the colour and the products, that makes it sound as if they have an option. It makes it sound as if you have two levels of service, awesome service and basic service, who wants anything that is basic?

You have to believe that people do not want basic, everybody wants their version of the best. Why do you think most people have five hundred TV channels, and pay hundreds of £/$ each year, why they do not settle for the basic eight?

Why do you think Costa coffee has a zillion options of coffee? Because no one really wants a basic coffee.

Basic does not make you feel good, make you feel aspirational, basic reminds you that you should have done better.

Nobody tells their friends "I am doing the worse I can, I am average, I am basic or I am at the bottom" It makes you feel as if you have settled for less, less than you want and less than you deserve.

> ## RESPECT YOURSELF
> "ONLY OTHER PEOPLE TELL YOU IT IS OKAY TO BE AT THE BOTTOM, USUALLY IT IS THE PEOPLE WHO ARE AT THE TOP."

If, and some clients will, ask "what is the price without the products? Just go ahead and tell them what the basic service costs. You are not closing the deal today (apart from the deposit or booking fee) you are just educating the client and selling the benefits.

You can have another go at selling and closing the client when they return, and it will be much easier this time.

THE PRODUCT FLOW STRUCTURE

Here are the Moves!

You need a predetermined physical flow that never gets changed. Unlike the verbal script, the flow is a discipline, it needs to become a habit. The flow will ensure that you never forget a single client, you cannot, ever break the flow.

Even if the same client was in yesterday you must follow the flow. Once you allow reasons to be applied to stop the flow the team will get creative at engineering new reasons for reducing product sales, until you end up back at the starting point of not selling.

The second reason for the flow is for the salon owner to know, without asking a single question if the selling process is in place. If a salon owner can walk the salon at any given time and see that the current client has the current products in from of them, they will know that the staff member at the back wash has done their job.

If the products end up on the reception desk, they will know that the stylist has done their job. If the receptionist puts the products in a bag and takes the money, they know that the team has done their job.

All this without even asking a single question.

> ## PRODUCT FLOW
> "THE PRODUCT FLOW MUST NEVER BE BROKEN, IT IS THE UNBREAKABLE COMMUNICATION LINK BETWEEN THE TEAM."

The different sectors in our industry will have different flows, but as an example a hair salon would have three main points of flow.

The reception, the backwash, the work station and then the reception again, so in this case a triangular flow.

Carl Hinder/Sell products or die (not) trying

This is what you need to do for your salon. This is your flow.

Reception: The receptionist should be like the conductor of an orchestra. When an orchestra has a conductor, they play fine music, without one they find it difficult to understand what the other sections are doing and eventually the overall quality drops. In my opinion a great, well trained receptionist is a much better asset to a salon on a daily basis than even a salon manager, who is stuck to the back of a chair. Where your business does not have a receptionist, it should be on your list to develop your business enough to have one. Your product sales alone could pay for a full-time receptionist, maybe two.

This book is not about reception training, but I will give you an outline of a typical operation. When your client arrives, they are normally greeted by the receptionist who should introduce themselves if the client is new, then confirm the service that they have booked in for, or the service that they would like, checking that the time and day are all correct. Once this is done the receptionist will take their coat and offer the client a seat, usually along with refreshments too. In larger premises, if time permits, I would expect the receptionist to offer a tour of the premises, paying specific attention to the services that the client may not be aware of and the retail area.

Carl Hinder/Sell products or die (not) trying

The stylist should be informed that their client has arrived for the specified service. If there is a time delay between client arrival and the stylist being available, this is a great opportunity for the receptionist to engage with the client, probably in the seated area. The receptionist needs to be on a fact finding mission, with the intention of finding out the clients future needs that will be largely non-hair related, probably addressing gift solutions. This is too early to close any deals, but you can open the dialogue. A birthday, "how wonderful, you should consider our gift vouchers, I am sure they would be thrilled, A Christmas gift, we have the most amazing hair straighteners, would you mind if I showed you?" You have to make this time work, and the receptionist has to contribute to the selling effort, just as much as any other member of staff.

The receptionist need a sales (performance) target too. So, they can be measured on gifts sold, gift vouchers sold, referral cards redeemed and upsells made. Whilst this is not largely part of the product selling culture or directly part of this book it is part of the customer service culture, and service through selling.

If you want to know more about setting targets for receptionists, please e mail me directly info@salon-help.co.uk, and I will send out a fact sheet.

Once the stylist is available, they should collect their client and either take them to the designated consultation area or to their workstation for the consultation. (Not the colour consultation, that is a separate service), once the stylist has finished the consultation, they or the junior can then escort the client to the backwash area. If the client has been told about any specific products on the phone the receptionist should refer to any notes and inform the junior and the Stylist.

We will of course return back to the reception area.

Backwash: Depending on your salon size you may well have a dedicated shampooing person, a junior or a stylist carrying out this service (or no one at all if you do not do hair). Whoever it is they have a key role, and very important salon responsibility. Assuming that the stylist has authorised the client to be shampooed then there are a few basic steps that need to be covered with the client.

If the stylist already knows what the client should be using or needs to use then they should verbally communicate that with the person shampooing, otherwise the person shampooing should ask the client:

"What shampoo do you currently use?"

Carl Hinder/Sell products or die (not) trying

This is important, as they may have purchased one from you recently and you do not want to contradict what another stylist has already recommended. If the client is being shampooed before a colour service then a simple every day or clarifying shampoo may be appropriate, but this is unlikely to be the recommendation.

Asking, open ended questions will allow the client to impart more information without them feeling like they are being interrogated. "How would you describe the condition of your hair?" or "How would you like your hair to feel? are simple and common questions. Please do not ask "How do you find your hair?" you are bound to get a response, "Err easily, it is always in the same place."

Once the shampooing and possibly conditioning process is complete you should escort the client to the work station where the stylist can take over, or if you are the stylist you can continue with the service.

Here is the KEY ACTION. Once the client is seated the person who did the shampooing needs to fetch the products that they have recommended from the retail stand and put them in front of the client at the work station, saying "these are the products that I recommended for you at the back wash". The client can choose to pick them up and ask further questions.

Carl Hinder/Sell products or die (not) trying

The stylist and the salon manager now know that the person who has done the shampoo has done their part of the flow. They have done their part in selling. The stylist now also knows what has been recommended without even asking. The stylist will normally continue with that recommendation, however, if the stylist feels the recommendation is wrong all they have to say is "the dedicated person doing the shampoo (name) is absolutely right about these products, but I think on this occasion this other item might work a little better".

Most salon and Barber backwashes will not have every product available to use, and therefore it may not reflect the range on display. This is why it is important to retrieve and present the products that you recommend not necessarily the products that you have used.

PRODUCT FLOW

"THE KEY TO PRODUCT FLOW IS MOVING THE PRODUCT TO WHERE EVER THE CLIENT GOES."

Work station: With the client now in the stylists chair the stylist can confirm what the clients has requested and highlight the process. Now is the time to start the product sell for the styling and finishing. Do not wait. This might sound over eager, but you are preparing the client for later on in the service. So, you can repeat "you are having an all over colour, a short choppy bob with a textured finish, (client acknowledges,) great, I have got the perfect mattifying powder for that, you are going to love it." End of product introduction.

Now it is time to ask questions, listen and learn about the colour, style, how they will maintain it. Holidays, job interviews and their social life. You may have to engage more with the client using more open-ended questions. You can then make your recommendation to solve those problems.

Typical but important questions could be:

"What do you already like about your hair?"

"What is it you do not like?"

"Tell me one thing you would change?"

"How have you been able to manage your hair at home since I saw you last?"

You should now be searching for the problem and identifying the solution. "Oh, you are going on holiday, let me tell you more about how to stop this colour fading while you are there." You can go on to describe your best colour leave in conditioner, explain the benefits, features and advantages of it to the client, and alleviate any doubts that they might have.

KEY ACTION. Go and collect (or ask someone) the item that you have just been describing and selling, and hand it to the client. "This is the product that I was just telling you about." That is all you need to do for now, do not keep repeating yourself.
Continue with the service until you get to styling and finishing, invariably this will need a product or two of some description.

Now, you can use the product that you mentioned very early in the process and produce the mattifying powder that is so amazing "here is that fantastic mattifying powder that I told you about earlier," tell the client about its features, advantages and benefits but no need to go over the top. This type of link selling works because the client knows that you are genuine, but more importantly passionate about the product. If you have bought into it, so will they!

> # LINK SELLING
> "MENTION THE PRODUCT VERY EARLY IN THE PROCESS, BUT YOU DO NOT PRODUCE IT UNTIL YOU ARE HALFWAY THROUGH THE SERVICE."

You can repeat this process as many times as you like until you have found solutions for all the clients problems, including their gift needs. All the items that are needed should be in front of the client, and **only** the items that they need should be there. Apart from these specific items, the work station shelf should be clear. Having these products in front of the client allows the salon owner to check that the stylist is performing the service as required, simply by looking and requires no verbal communication.

Once the service is complete the stylist should escort the client to the desk.

KEY ACTION take the products that have been recommended from the work station and put them on the reception desk in front of the client. If the stylist remains at the desk to complete the transaction, they should ask the client.

1) "Which of these products would you like to take with you today?

Carl Hinder/Sell products or die (not) trying

If they only choose one item, then you need to follow up with another question.

2) "Is one going to be enough?"

THIS IS THE CLOSE. IF YOU DO NOT ASK THE QUESTION YOU WILL NOT KNOW THE ANSWER. IF YOU DO NOT CLOSE THERE IS NO POINT IN DOING ANYTHING ELSE WITH THIS BOOK.

If the client is being handing over to the receptionist, then the receptionist knows what the stylist has recommended without any verbal communication, because the products are in front of them both. If the stylist is not at hand the receptionist should say.

1) "Your stylist (name) has recommended these for you, which ones would you like to take with you today?"

If they only choose one item, then you need to follow up with another question.

2) "Is one going to be enough?"

Because the products are on the desk, the salon owner can again see, and hear that the flow system is working without having to ask any questions.

There is a general saying, in that the second sale is easier than the first one. This means that if the client agrees to purchase a product, possibly a shampoo, they have bought into you and everything you have said, so asking if the client would like the conditioner to go with it should be an automatic process, which will give a high success rate. This is a firm closing statement, but one that can be delivered in a pleasant manner.

Asking "would you like a shampoo today?" does not work, at least not often enough. Please do not say this.

You can create your own flows and scripts if you are in a clinic, spa or other industry outlet. The key point is that products should be lightly suggested early, enforced during the service and the physical product must follow the client around the room until it arrives at the point of sale.

CLOSE THE SALE
"IF YOU DO NOT ASK THE QUESTION, YOU WILL NOT KNOW THE ANSWER"

MARKETING

Marketing is just the vehicle that you use to deliver your message (your advert).

Selling starts before the salon even opens. If you are serious about selling products, and by now you should be all in with this plan, then selling yourself, your salon and your products should be at every opportunity.

Before you start on any marketing products, it is important to remember why clients are going to ultimately buy them. **The client buys a product once the value of the item exceeds the price.**

The value of an item is measured by the level of benefit that the client believes they will get from the product, including how it makes them feel.

To know how and what you are marketing you need to write down all the problems that a typical client might NEED you to solve. You list might include, anything from colour fade to weight control, dry skin to wrinkles, or dandruff to brittle nails. The list can be as long as you want. All your marketing materials should then be focused on the problem you are solving, and the result that the client will benefit from and feel.

The more emotional attachment that you attach to the 'feeling' the more you will connect and the more you will sell.

As an example: someone might have wrinkles at the sides or above their eyes, giving them a look, older than their years. This can often affect their confidence too. Your marketing would focus on the benefits of Botox, how quick (benefit) easy (benefit) convenient (benefit) and painless (feeling) the treatment is. How it makes you look younger (feeling), feel younger (feeling), gives you more confidence (feeling). When done in conjunction with our 'awesome skin care kit', the effect will last for months longer (benefit), keeping you looking youthful (feeling) and giving you a skin tone, you only ever dreamt of (big feeling) and keeping the new you for longer (feeling). No matter what you are charging, when you have this much benefit and positive emotion the price will not matter, they just want to be that person. This is the level of marketing that you must find. Just putting an image of someone being injected with Botox and a sign underneath saying 'Botox now only £/$100.00 per course will get you nowhere at all.

This is the style of marketing that you need to follow throughout. Benefit and Feeling.

This is not a book on salon marketing, but let us have an overview:

DIGITAL MARKETING

Let us, start with social media, the most over used and poorly executed marketing tool that you have. For most salons, social media is a disaster and is no more effective for them than standing with your back to a wishing well and throwing a coin over your shoulder. This is usually because salon owners do not actually know enough about the ways in which to use social media, but also because of image saturation. Firstly, do not keep posting standard images of before and after haircuts, colours, nails, eye brows and whatever other services you provide. The internet is knee high in billions of these images, and on their own they perform poorly. Do not get caught up in the make-believe world of engagements, likes, shares and members, if they do not turn up at your salon someday all these figures mean nothing at all.

The biggest mismanagement of social media that business' make is that they have forgotten the SOCIAL part of Social Media. This means engaging with other people, and people usually engage with other people who they have an interest in.

When you use social media platforms in your business give the client, or potential client a reason to identify with you socially. Tell them more about you and your business and how they can engage or share in your business or your story.

To do this with products you must replicate the salon experience and that means educating the client. So yes, you may well have the most amazing hair style as your lead picture, in the same image frame you will have the product(s) that created it, and a small punchy description of what the product has done and how it could benefit your audience. Do not try and sell the product there and then. Give the potential client something to do, follow this link, come for a free consultation, join us for a coffee morning, but do not sell just yet.

As is now the norm, video content is expected, and indeed much more effective than a still image. Make your videos inclusive of the products and do reviews, education and testimonials using video and live video content. Include the service and the product used in every video.

All your advertising needs to include a product reference, new products, innovative products, products that will solve problems for clients.

Look at product competitions, free product giveaways (get the supplier to help), just make sure the clients come in to the salon to collect their prize and always get them to stay for a coffee. Now it is time to sell, it is time to sell yourself.

Staying with digital, when you send out news letters or e mail reminders, have a product related reference on them, you do not need to do the sale at this point, just the awareness. Essentially as you are retraining the client on the value of using great products.

MARKETING

"MARKETING IS THE VEHICLE THAT YOU USE TO CARRY THE MESSAGE, WHICH WE CALL ADVERTISING."

Your website needs to reflect your product selling, customer service ethos. Do not hide your products away under a tab so that people have to look for them, make it graphically clear that you have the best products for their needs, use a blog or vlog feature to write about them, record videos and recycle them on your social media too. You have to be obsessed with the value of customer service through product selling.

Ideally, though not essential, you could do with having an e commerce shop with your website, so that you can sell online, particularly for clients who want extra items in between visits.

To ensure that they use the page, organise a points reward scheme for the products so that your clients do not stray to another site. Of course you should have your own brand range by then, so they will not be able to get those products anywhere else.

Product selling is not just something that you do at reception in the last few minutes after a service. You can manage your clients homecare needs, everyday 24/7 if you utilise all the tools available to you. **Whichever method you use, it only really matters when you close the deal.**
Important Note

Social media is an exceptionally powerful tool which salon owners must embrace and secure training on, without social media your business is at a massive disadvantage. But you must learn to use it properly.

Carl Hinder/Sell products or die (not) trying

P2P: PERSON TO PERSON

We are a person to person (P2P) business model, and whilst all the digital marketing is essential in our business, the power of face to face interaction is almost immeasurable. Indeed, it is my opinion that the less we interact as humans the more powerful face to face communication will become. Getting yourself in front to people is the best way, bar none to sell yourself. With that in mind having salon events for new product launches, demonstrations and social events will drive your ability to sell more products and develop your customer service. Coffee mornings and open evenings will give you and your team the opportunity to demonstrate to potential clients, your facilities, knowledge and product solutions. Utilise all the social events that you can to drive new clientele into your business and educate them on products at an early stage, but remember the important process continues to happen on a daily basis in the salon with every client that visits you.

COMMUNICATE IN PERSON

"AS DIGITAL COMMUNICATION GROWS, PERSON TO PERSON COMMUNICATION BECOMES MORE POWERFUL."

I have already given you an insight into the opportunities to market yourselves within the salon, at the reception area or when carrying out consultations earlier in this book. Due to the importance of these areas, it is essential that I re-iterate the focus that you need to apply.

Reception: when a client makes an appointment by phone, we should now be taking this opportunity to market. Not only should we be trading them up in services, but we should now be telling the client about the new product to look out for when they come in. So if a regular colour client books in by phone then we should say, with energy "I am so glad you have booked your colour service in, we have just had a new colour treatment arrive this week, I will make sure your stylist (by name) shows them to you when you come in", have the product ready for the stylist to discuss on the day!

The consultation: There are two types of consultation,

- a) The sit down, lets understand the clients circumstances in depth and tailor the service to them. Ideal, and usually reserved for colour clients, clients that have long term skin treatments, microblading, colonic irrigation etc.

Carl Hinder/Sell products or die (not) trying

I call these the slow down and speed up sessions. Slowing down the consultation usually speeds up the service and product selling.

These consultations need to be documented. Discovering what your clients problems, needs and expectations are, will ensure that your client can be serviced quickly, smoothly and have a fantastic service experience. During these sessions you need to address their product requirements in detail. If it is a colour consultation you need to get the products that the client will need to maintain and style their hair. It will probably be between three and six products. Go through each one, explaining why you will be using it and the benefits to the client, write them down on your consultation form. Do not try and make a sale today!

The same with other services like colonic irrigation or hydrotherapy. You will go through the clients reasons for the service, the benefits they will have, describe the process and of course the health benefits. To aid the health benefits you will have dietary and nutritional supplements available that the client will benefit from and of course need. Get these items out, describe what they do, the benefits and how they can get them. Write them on the consultation form. Do not try and make a sale today!

b) Where the consultation is more casual, maybe just before the hair cut or the nail service, you still need the discussion, but instead of writing down the recommendation, just repeat the problems that they have told you, back to them, and tell them what you will be using today, and how that will benefit them. Short pieces of information, not a lecture. Do not try and sell yet, the consultations are all about fact finding, identifying the problems, educating the client and finding the issue. Deposits, or booking charges aside you are not looking to close the sale on products during the consultation. This is all marketing, your services and your products.

You are building up the trust.

PART 5: HOW DO I REALLY SELL?

THE RELATIONSHIP

If you have just opened this book and have started reading from this page, you will fail.

Go back to the beginning to fully understand all of the barriers that will prevent you from succeeding.

If you have read parts 1-4 then you now have most of the pieces in place for a serious change in your business, which I promise will also change your life, if you are dedicated to customer service through product sales.

Even though every individual in an organisation has to take responsibility for themselves it will be the power of the team that makes this work, unless you work on your own of course, then everything is down to you.

I have already established for you that clients who fail to buy are doing so, because you the stylist or business owner has not done something. You failed to tell the client something that was important to them. Even though we have put structures in place to help you manage product sales performance, this is not a paint by numbers exercise. You cannot apply the same sales pitch to every client, that would just demonstrate that you are not listening.

However, when you start out you do need a script, certainly for the first few weeks until you start to feel more natural in educating your client and handling rejections.

Your relationship with the client is paramount to successful selling, but that does not have to be a mutually friendly relationship, it has to be a mutually respectful relationship. The client does not need to like you immediately to buy from you, they need to know you, understand you and trust you. However, people like people and being a likeable person will make your job a lot easier. You should do everything that you can to make the client like you. Do this and you will definitely be more successful at convincing your clients to buy. This means that what you are selling is you. You are selling yourself to the client, the product sale will follow.

Professionals in our industry are great at talking and usually poor at listening. You are great at engaging in long social discussion, but never hear when the client is telling you they have a need. When a client tells you, they are going on holiday your ears should channel the information to your brain that the client needs a top up tan, a chlorine protecting conditioner, a sun block, a travel straightening iron, a small tin of wax, a shave before they leave etc.

Carl Hinder/Sell products or die (not) trying

At all times you should be saying to the client (or rather to yourself) I am going to find your problem, I am going to solve your problem, I am going to make you look amazing and I am going to tell you how to stay looking amazing. Think about this, does a client really want a haircut, nails, Botox, massage or eyelashes? Do clients actually want these things? The answer is no, they want these things because of what those things do. They make the client feel good, maybe confident. If this feeling was not attached to the purchase, they would not have it. The same with a product, it has to make them feel as if there is a benefit to them. Once you can show that the benefit and the feeling they get from having it is big enough, they will buy. Learn these things and you will be a great success as a salon owner, a stylist and as a seller. You have already bought into yourself and the product, so you are nearly there.

Being positive at all times is essential. Think about it, does a client want to go to a positive stylist or the negative miserable stylist? Is that positive stylist you? Is there even a positive stylist in your salon? If that positive stylist is a little further down the street, where do you think that client will eventually end up?

The most powerful tool that you have available for clients who have objections is agreement. You must agree with any objections that a client says to you. If you disagree with them, they will not buy your product, even if your objection is perfectly right. You have to think about this in terms of your life; if someone shouts at you, you feel like shouting back at them, even if you are only shouting "DO NOT SHOUT AT ME!" If someone waves at you, you want to wave back, and it is a known fact that if someone smiles at you, you will smile back, and if someone disagrees with you, you will normally disagree back. When you disagree with a client, the focus is now on the disagreement, not on the product or service any longer. By agreeing with a clients objection, you are still in the conversation and you now have the next move.

AGREEMENT

"NEVER DISAGREE WITH A CLIENT, EVER. ALWAYS AGREE WITH THEM, EVEN WHEN YOU KNOW THEY ARE WRONG."

You do not have to agree verbatim, if a client says your products are too expensive, you do not say "yes, they are too expensive". That will kill the conversation.

Carl Hinder/Sell products or die (not) trying

You say "Yes (agree), I hear what you are saying, but when you think it lasts three months, that is pretty good?" if a client says "I can get that product cheaper on the internet," you do not say "yes you can" you say "yes (agree), I have heard someone say that before," but, did you know that we have this product made only for us, so what you are getting is pretty special."

If a client says, "I can shave at home, quicker and cheaper," You do not say "Yes I know, that is why most men do." You say "Yes (agree) sure, but have you ever had a hot towel shave with a master barber, you will feel like a King."

As we looked at in the 'reasons for not selling section' earlier in the book, it was rejection that was stopping you from selling and delivering the best service. For most stylists being told NO is taken as a personal rejection. When, in reality a no answer is usually because you have just not given the client some kind of information that makes them see that the product is more important/desirable that the money that they give you in exchange. Because you get a few rejections you cannot reduce your effort, you cannot worry that you are doing the wrong things, because the natural thing to do then is nothing, and doing nothing is not going to improve the client experience.

Next time you get a no, a rejection or just simply fail to sell (close) write it down. Get a diary and write down all your rejections. Every day, when you have a quiet period grab ahold of the product champion, the salon owner, another member of staff or at least, stand in the mirror. Discuss, think and challenge yourself, what could I say next time? Write it down. Get a big diary there will be an awful lot of rejections.

Do not avoid rejections, otherwise you will retract, you will fail to sell and fail to give the best ever service. If you are telling the truth about a product, and you should not be saying anything else but the truth, you should be feeling good about yourself.

Learning how to improve customer service through selling takes a lot of dedication and training. It is not a one-off training session, it is a daily, weekly and monthly obsession. Whilst books like this will persuade you to change your business model, and there are online courses available at www.salon-help.co.uk to help too, but the real development comes from within the business. You need to be videoing your techniques and responses, reviewing them and changing them, as a group or even on your own. Changing one small piece can have a dramatic effect on your performance.

EPILOGUE / CONCLUSION

Customer service, and that always means including the product, is the only way to beat your competition. We know that historically salons do not, and often will not sell products, and they will continue to under achieve. Customer service is the only way to beat the competition, you cannot beat them on a service, one haircut is largely the same as another (at least to the client), and you cannot beat them on price because people with less respect for their time and their lives will always do less, and always get in the race to the bottom. Customer service is the only place where you can win, nobody has you or your team, your drive, enthusiasm or great ideas.

Do not worry about selling products, worry that your customer service standards are poor, and you will then sell products. Do not sell the client a product, sell them an experience, you know that the client just cannot have the full experience without the product.

This book only exists because of our need to generate money as a parent, as part of society and as a business. It is your duty to yourself and everyone around you to generate as much money as you can, utilising all the skills that you have.

Sure, there are people outside the realms of material society, living in communities outside of ours. I wish them well and they are unlikely to ever read this book. However, if you are a business owner, self-employed or employed you are part of society that depends on you doing as much as you can, contributing as much as you can. Whether you want to or not, you pay taxes, the more money you can generate the more investment into society you can make.

Within this society most people that I have ever met want success in one form or another, most want to measure that success with the amount of money they have or for the things they have exchanged for that money. The way that most salon owners approach success and money is with an attitude that success and money are an optional part of running their business. It is as if they do a set of tasks, they might get lucky, and if it happens it would be great. If it happens it happens, if it does not happen, well I can just keep going or try something else. I guarantee that if that is your loose attitude to success, your next business will fail too. Accepting failure is worse than failure itself. When you fail you can learn from it, you can hate it, you can use it as motivation, but accepting failure means that you are not changing and if you are not changing then your results are likely to always be the same.

Carl Hinder/Sell products or die (not) trying

The barrier to success is you (serious ill health and death aside), you do not make enough effort, you do not work hard enough, and I mean you do not work hard enough doing the things that are difficult to overcome. You chose to do only the things that you like, the things that you enjoy and the things that you are comfortable with. The more comfortable you are, the less success you will have, and the longer you feel comfortable the quicker any success that you did have will drain away. You will not get anywhere near your dreams, your ambitions and your goals by only doing the things that you like.

In most countries success and financial wealth are scorned and frowned upon by the people who are only prepared to do the minimum, and they, themselves get minimum results. You really are not going to get anywhere trying to take the shortest route to success, you need to take the most appropriate route, the one that gives you the best chance, no matter how difficult the route is. The super wealthy in our society have overcome all the obstacles in their way, especially the hardest ones of all, the ones that they put in place themselves. We envy them, yet we say we despise them, we loath them instead of learning from them.

Would success really be a negative thing for you and your family?

What happens next?

I am guessing you will read the book once, and seeing as you have got this far, I know that you are serious about improving your customer service and selling products. I also know that you will be telling yourself that you do not agree with everything I have told you, and that is okay too. When you have to make changes this radical there are always reservations.

You will feel conflicted, knowing that you need to do everything in this book to make your salon a success. You may well feel as if you cannot do it or you are not prepared to do it. Both could result in the same outcome for you and your business, at best a mediocre business, at worse a declining business, or a business that will never reach its potential.

The result of what you achieve is directly proportional to the effort you put in. Huge, obsessive, undeterred effort will result in success. No effort will result in NOTHING.

Your next job is to read this book again, this time with a note book and pen at hand.

Carl Hinder/Sell products or die (not) trying

Identify all the action points that you and your team need to start making, and write them down in an order that makes sense to you. Getting your team, a copy of this book will also make the changes smoother because they will know what will be required of them, and they will know that it is not personal. (It is my fault, not yours).

Maybe you feel that you need more support, well I have plenty for you. Salon Help also has an online course which you and each member of your team can work through. Most of the course is video supported so everything in the book and more, is explained clearly.

Just go to www.salon-help.co.uk

The course also has a bonus module which is not in this book. This module is on advanced selling techniques that will lift your service and your sales up another level again. The module is not complicated, it can be a lot of fun getting it right with your team, but it does need a little bit of sales experience and a definite commitment to selling products for you to get the best

Alternately, you can go to www.salon-help.co.uk and "reserve a time" with me on our booking system and I will talk you through the book and any specific issues that you have or areas that you want help to develop.

You can apply most of the rules and guidance in this book to selling anything in your business, whether it is a product, a service or yourself. Let us start with selling customer service through product sales and see where that takes us, I bet it is to a better place. Watch as other salons around you struggle and close, whilst holding the firm belief that selling products is a terrible thing. I very much doubt that their family is as happy as you and your family.

Thank you for buying my book and joining me on my crusade to change the world of retailing in our industry in the UK and across the world.

BIBLIOGRAPHY

"Propaganda." (2010). In: Oxford Dictionary. Oxford University Press

"Sell." (2010). In: Oxford Dictionary. Oxford University Press

ACKNOWLEDGMENTS

You have to thank people who have made you the person that you are, but greater thanks go to the people that can make you the person that you can become.

The most influential manager of my time, and probably my first mentor was Colin Whittaker, store manager in ASDA superstore Farnborough, Hampshire. Colin might have been the last of the traditional traders. A man who knew how to retail, how to remove the shackles that bind us and how to be enterprising. He drove me to despair and perfection in equal measures, he kept his business in focus and my development in line. I feared his wrath and appreciated his compassion. Colin, I do not know if you are still with us on earth, but thank you, wherever you are.

Being married to an entrepreneur is not easy for anyone, but for the past twenty years my wife Tina has been there when the ship needed steadying, and when I needed to get through another business storm. She knows my obsession for perfection, and that the next big development is only a sleep away, but she never derails me and believes in me. I never have to compromise, and she would never let me be less than I can be. She makes me a better coach and a better person every day. Thankyou Tina, but the ride is not over yet.

Carl Hinder/Sell products or die (not) trying

ABOUT THE AUTHOR

Carl Hinder, Director of Salon Help Business Coaching is a business coach, mentor, trainer, public speaker and author. He is known as an influencer, and for his tough, no excuses approach to getting businesses to change and develop. Now based back in Wales (UK), outside of Cardiff. Whilst living in London and the South East of England, the author spent twenty years working in the retail sector with some of the top retailers in the UK. Managerial roles across clothing, electrical, food and DIY operations has given the author a wide business perspective, in operations ranging from £/$35k to £/$1m a week.

With a family background in the health and beauty industry it was inevitable that the author would revisit the industry that he grew up in. During the late 1990's the author launched a salon chain that would define his career path for the next twenty years. His inclination towards networking led him to become the secretary and later the President for the National Hairdressers Federation in Wales. He was instrumental in re-establishing the Welsh hairdressing championships and the Welsh hairdressing awards, as well as other key events in the Principality.

The authors unique business background in the corporate and salon environment has meant that he is always in demand with serious business owners across the UK and the USA, engaging them with his analytical, controversial and thorough style of management. Having coached business teams and salons throughout his career the author formally established Salon Help in 2015, with an emphasis on one to one coaching. Identifying the growth in the industry he now provides, books, video coaching, online courses and a free online video phone in service.

He shares his business passion with his love of motorcycles, occasionally combining the two and getting the most from life. He is dedicated to his work and to his wife Tina, and children Ffion and Morgan.

SUMMARY POINTS

Summary Points:

- You must change the way you think about product selling

- You need to forget the old excuses

- You must remember that there are more reasons for selling than there are for failing

- You must not accept any barriers from anyone

- You must accept product sales as customer service

- You must be obsessed with product selling

- You must understand that selling is a normal human process

- You must understand that the client should come before your own fears.

- You must not separate products from customer service.

Carl Hinder/Sell products or die (not) trying

ACTION POINTS

ACTION POINTS

- Read this book

- Read it again but now have a pad and pen to write things down

- From section one — INTRODUCTION AND SELLING

    Write down in one word what this book is about.

    1)

Carl Hinder/Sell products or die (not) trying

- From section two — WHY YOU SHOULD SELL

    Write down the main reasons that product selling would benefit you or your client. Write down at least four reasons:

    1)

    2)

    3)

    4)

    5)

    6)

Carl Hinder/Sell products or die (not) trying

- From section three — Myths and excuses

    Write down the main reasons that you have used, told yourself or heard other team members using. Write down at least four excuses:

    1)

    2)

    3)

    4)

    5)

    6)

- From section four — How to make changes

    Write down the key changes that you or your team need to make urgently. You may need to do this for each member of the team and not just the overall salon.

    Write down at least four changes:

    1)

    2)

    3)

    4)

    5)

    6)

Carl Hinder/Sell products or die (not) trying

- From section five — How do I really sell

    Write down the most important rule when you are having a discussion. What should you never do ?

    1)

    Lastly — Now write down how many products you sold last month and divide it by four write that number here.

    (   )

    E mail me that number to info@salon-help.co.uk

    I will be in contact in six months time to see how well you are doing.

    Good luck, the business is now back in your hands.

Carl Hinder/Sell products or die (not) trying

Carl Hinder/Sell products or die (not) trying

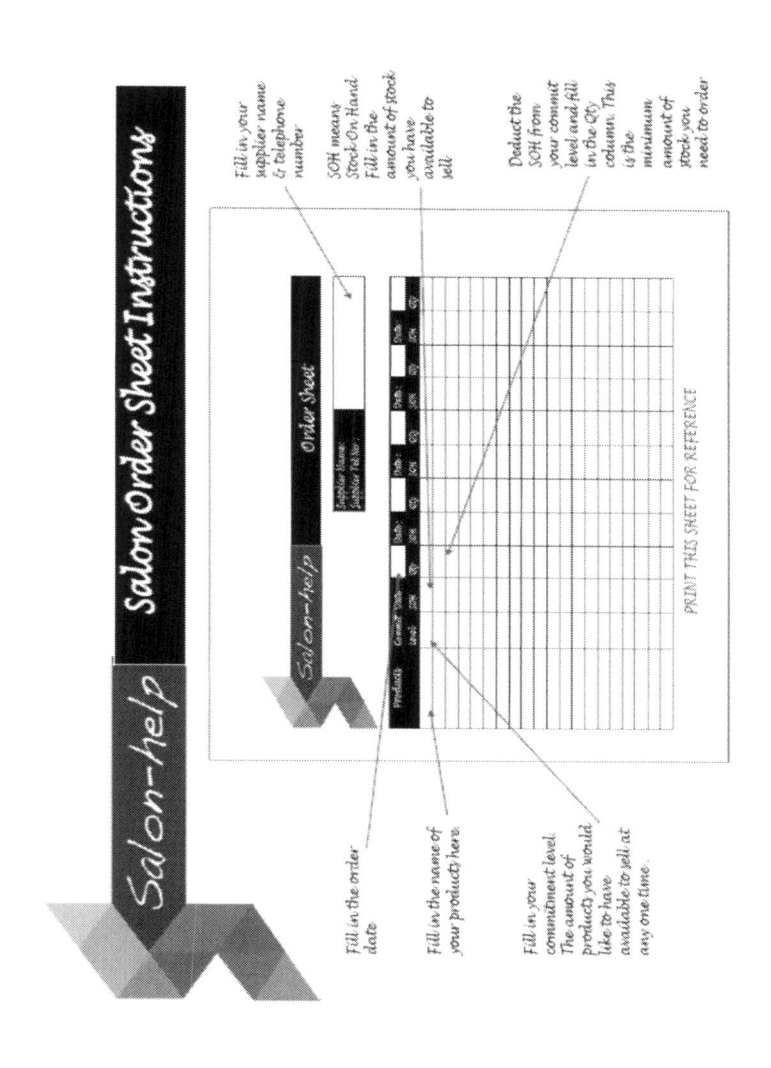

Salon Order Sheet Instructions

Order Sheet

- Fill in the order date
- Fill in the name of your products here.
- Fill in your commitment level. The amount of products you would like to have available to sell at any one time.
- Fill in your supplier name & telephone number
- SOH means Stock On Hand. Fill in the amount of stock you have available to sell
- Deduct the SOH from you commit level and fill in the Qty column. This is the minimum amount of stock you need to order

PRINT THIS SHEET FOR REFERENCE

227

CUSTOMER SERVICE RECORD SHEET

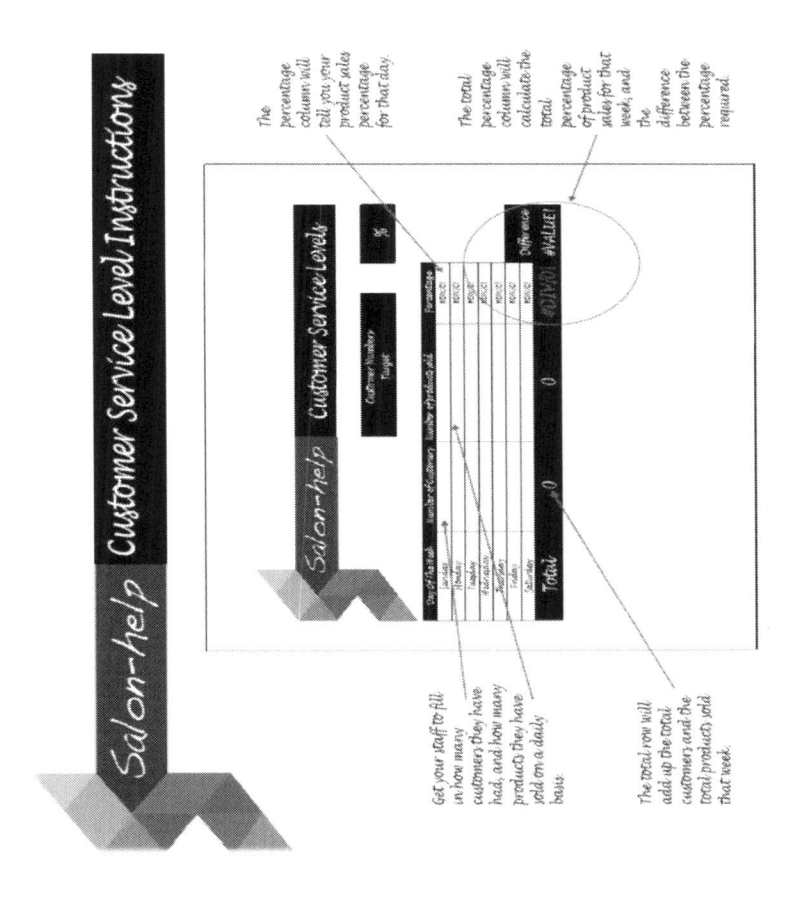

Feel free to email me and I will send you these to print off and fill in.

Printed in Great Britain
by Amazon